AFGHAN
PEACE TALKS

A PRIMER

JAMES SHINN, JAMES DOBBINS

D0104350

NATIONAL SECURITY
RESEARCH DIVISION

This publication results from the RAND Corporation's Investment in People and Ideas program. Support for this program is provided, in part, by the generosity of RAND's donors and by the fees earned on client-funded research.

Library of Congress Cataloging-in-Publication Data

Shinn, James.
  Afghan peace talks : a primer / James Shinn, James Dobbins.
    p. cm.
  Includes bibliographical references.
  ISBN 978-0-8330-5819-5 (pbk. : alk. paper)
    1. Peace-building—Afghanistan. 2. Afghan War, 2001—Peace. 3. Diplomatic negotiations in international disputes. I. Dobbins, James, 1942- II. Title.

  JZ5584.A33S55 2011
  958.104'71—dc23

                                                                2011030896

The RAND Corporation is a nonprofit institution that helps improve policy and decisionmaking through research and analysis. RAND's publications do not necessarily reflect the opinions of its research clients and sponsors.
RAND® is a registered trademark.

Cover image of President Hamid Karzai courtesy of AP Photo (Musadeq Sadeq).

Published 2011 by the RAND Corporation
1776 Main Street, P.O. Box 2138, Santa Monica, CA 90407-2138
1200 South Hayes Street, Arlington, VA 22202-5050
4570 Fifth Avenue, Suite 600, Pittsburgh, PA 15213-2665
RAND URL: http://www.rand.org/
To order RAND documents or to obtain additional information, contact
Distribution Services: Telephone: (310) 451-7002;
Fax: (310) 451-6915; Email: order@rand.org

Preface

In early 2010, when the authors began to participate in exploratory discussions, under the auspices of The Century Foundation, regarding the possibility of a negotiated peace in Afghanistan, the very concept of talking to the enemy was controversial in official circles and little discussed beyond them. The objective of a negotiated peace has since been firmly embraced by both the Afghan and American governments, supported by the North Atlantic Treaty Organization, and endorsed by most of Afghanistan's neighbors. Taliban intermediaries have held talks on the subject with both Afghan and American officials. As this monograph makes clear, we are still some distance from full-scale negotiations, let alone a peace settlement, but the exploratory process has clearly passed from former officials and academic observers, such as ourselves, into more-authoritative hands.

This monograph is the product of the our personal experience in dealing with Afghanistan and other trouble spots and of conversations held over the past 18 months with many potential participants in any Afghan peace process, including senior Afghan officials, leading members of the Afghan parliamentary opposition and civil society, former and current Taliban figures, and representatives of the many governments likely to play a role in any such peace process, whether directly or behind the scenes. Our purpose is to provide a guide, for both officials and observers, to the conduct of such negotiations as they may evolve over the next several years.

This monograph is a product of the RAND Corporation's continuing program of self-initiated independent research. Support for such research is provided, in part, by donors and by the independent research and development provisions of RAND's contracts for the operation of its U.S. Department of Defense federally funded research and development centers. The research was conducted within the RAND National Security Research Division (NSRD). NSRD conducts research and analysis on defense and national security topics for the U.S. and allied defense, foreign policy, homeland security, and intelligence communities and foundations and other nongovernmental organizations that support defense and national security analysis.

For more information on NSRD, see http://www.rand.org/nsrd/ or contact the director (contact information is provided on the web page).

Contents

Figures

Summary

The overarching American objective in Afghanistan should not simply be to prevent that country from becoming a haven for transnational terrorists but also to prevent it from becoming a terrorist ally. Prior to the attacks of September 11, 2001, Afghanistan was both a haven for and an ally of terrorists, and it would be so again if the Taliban returned to power with Al Qaeda backing. The United States can prevent this indefinitely as long as it is willing to commit significant military and economic resources to a counterinsurgency effort. It cannot eliminate the threat, however, as long as the Afghan insurgents enjoy sanctuary in and support from Pakistan. The United States could also achieve its objective if the Taliban could be persuaded to cut ties with Al Qaeda and end its insurgency in exchange for some role in Afghan governance short of total control.

Peace negotiations would obviously be desirable if they could succeed in achieving this objective, but they are also worth pursuing even if they fail, as the risks associated with entering such a process may be greater for the insurgents than for the Afghan government and its allies. The Taliban leadership is fighting a jihad [holy war] with a view to reimposing a religiously based form of government rooted in an extreme interpretation of Islam. Engaging in negotiations for something short of that goal undercuts the purity of that message. The Kabul regime, in contrast, is fighting for representative government (as well as its own survival and hold on power), and it is prepared to accept insurgent participation in government in some capacity if the insurgents lay down their arms. Opinion polling shows both overwhelming support within Afghan society for a negotiated settlement and a willingness to bring the Taliban back into the fold in something short of a dominant position. So, negotiating the terms of that entry with the Taliban is in no way inconsistent with the cause that the Kabul government espouses.

These considerations help explain why President Hamid Karzai, President Barack Obama, and leaders of other North Atlantic Treaty Organization (NATO) member countries have, in principle, endorsed peace negotiations while the insurgent leadership has remained much more circumspect. Nevertheless, conversations between a number of independent observers (including the authors) on one hand and Taliban representatives and those close to them on the other indicate serious insurgent interest in the possibility of a negotiated settlement. The recent death of Osama Bin Laden may help motivate Taliban leaders in two respects: first, making them more anxious about their own security and, second, perhaps removing whatever personal link there may have been between those leaders and Bin Laden. The latter may make it easier for the Taliban leaders to cut their remaining ties to Al Qaeda, a key American and NATO demand.

Getting the Afghan parties together is a necessary but not sufficient condition for a meaningful peace process. Afghanistan is a weak country surrounded by stronger neighbors. Historically, it has been at peace when its neighbors perceive a common interest in keeping that peace but at war—civil war—when one or more of those neighbors sees some advantage therein. Over the past 30 years, India, Iran, Pakistan, Russia, Saudi Arabia, and the United States have successfully supported insurgencies designed to overthrow the regime in Kabul. At present, it is Pakistan (and, to a much lesser degree, Iran) that is affording shelter and support to such an insurgency. Afghanistan will not be at peace until the governments of all of these countries see a common interest in that peace. To succeed, any peace process must therefore include these countries in some fashion.

Close examination reveals that the priorities of all the potential parties to an Afghan peace process overlap to a considerable degree. For instance, each desires a withdrawal of Western armed forces—a situation especially desired by the publics in all of the Western countries. All

Afghans want foreigners to stop interfering in their affairs. All foreign governments want assurances that Afghan territory will not be used to their disadvantage, whether by third parties or the Afghans themselves, and thus want to ensure that terrorists hostile to their countries cannot use Afghanistan as a sanctuary. Interests diverge less in the area of outcomes than in the area of timing. Western governments, under pressure from voters, want to withdraw NATO forces from Afghanistan (or at least from combat there) sooner rather than later, a preference shared by the Taliban leadership. Most other potential participants, including the Kabul government, are not in such a rush. Indeed, continuation of the current conflict, with the United States tied down and neither side able to prevail, is acceptable to most regional governments and, for Iran, probably optimal.

Negotiation among the Afghans will focus on the nature of any power-sharing arrangement, on possible modifications to the existing constitution, on social norms, and on the role of sharia law. Given the excessively centralized nature of the current Afghan government, it is not impossible that negotiations might actually lead to some improvement, via devolution, in subnational governance, although this would require both the Taliban leadership and the Kabul regime to alter their historical preference for a unitary, Kabul-centric system.

The American objective in these negotiations should be a stable and peaceful Afghanistan that neither hosts nor collaborates with international terrorists. Only to the extent that other issues impinge on this objective should American negotiators be drawn into a discussion of Afghanistan's social or constitutional issues. That qualification is significant, however, because constitutional issues will certainly affect Afghanistan's stability, as may social provisions if they are likely to antagonize influential elements of the population. In the end, however, the country's form of government and codes of behavior are preeminently of interest to the Afghans. Americans and other international actors should have some confidence that a reasonably representative Afghan government delegation will not stray far from the desires of its population, the overwhelming majority of whom are strongly opposed to a return of an Islamic emirate and desirous of retaining the many social and material gains most of them have made since 2001.

American and European opinion is, nevertheless, likely to be particularly sensitive to the issues of civil society and the role of women. However, the elements of Western society most concerned about such issues are also, in general, those least supportive of continued military engagement and thus the most likely to support unilateral steps that will reduce the negotiating leverage of both Washington and Kabul. This will lead to considerable dissonance in Western attitudes toward an enfolding peace process.

Other actors are likely to experience even greater dissonance. Neither the Kabul regime nor the Taliban is a well-integrated polity with a clear and reasonably unified sense of its respective interests and goals. Pakistani society may be even more divided than Afghan society, and the government in Islamabad often seems even less coherent than the one in Kabul, since the Pakistani political leadership and military establishment are autonomous actors with quite divergent priorities regarding domestic and foreign militancy and an Afghan settlement. Historically, the Pakistani military has employed militant groups and terrorism as instruments of policy. The country's civilian leadership seems convinced that this distinction between "good" and "bad" militants cannot be sustained now that the latter threaten the viability of the country's democracy. In contrast, the Pakistani military does not yet seem ready to cut ties with the terrorist groups with which it has long been associated. One of the main obstacles to any negotiated settlement will be getting the respective parties in Islamabad (and elsewhere) to decide what they really want and what they are willing to trade for it.

Herding such cats will strain the capacity of even the most skilled statesmen. As by far the most powerful and influential participant, the United States will have to play a leading role in this effort. But the United States is also one of the main protagonists in this conflict and therefore not in the best position to mediate. We thus recommend that Washington work to secure the appointment of a figure of international repute with the requisite impartiality, knowledge, contacts, and diplomatic skills to take charge of putting together and then orchestrating a multitiered negotiation process, one with the Afghans at its core as well as several concentric rings of regional and other interested governments actively but quietly engaged on the periphery.

Signaling and timing obviously matter a great deal in any peace process. The United States is due to begin withdrawing troops in mid-2011, and, with this withdrawal, its leverage in any negotiation will slowly diminish. Of all the possible major participants, therefore, the United States is likely to feel the greatest sense of urgency. Yet, its prospects of getting an acceptable agreement depend heavily on it not *needing* one. Only if Washington has an acceptable non-negotiated outcome in prospect will American diplomats have much chance of securing their negotiating objectives. This uncomfortable paradox accounts for much of the dissent and confusion in the American domestic debate on strategy in Afghanistan.

American policymakers must prepare for two futures: one negotiated, one not. Both must meet its bottom-line need to prevent Afghanistan from falling into the hands of an Al Qaeda–linked regime. This means preparing both to stay indefinitely and to go definitively. If negotiations fail, some level of American military engagement will probably be necessary well beyond the 2014 date by which President Obama has promised to remove all American combat forces. On the other hand, the full withdrawal of American troops from the country by some not-so-distant date is probably a necessary component of any peace deal. In bargaining terms, promising to leave is the American counterpart to the Taliban's commitment to cut its ties with Al Qaeda. Troubling as Americans may find this symmetry, these potential concessions represent each side's highest cards and are thus likely to be played only at the culmination of any negotiation process. Indeed, they will probably be essential to closing any deal.

It is thus perfectly reasonable for Washington and Kabul to be negotiating, as they are, the text of a long-term strategic partnership that involves an enduring military component. Without the prospect of such an enduring American presence, the Taliban would have little incentive to negotiate rather than just wait the United States and NATO out. On the other hand, American and Afghan officials should also be making clear, at least privately and perhaps publicly, that any such accord between Kabul and Washington is subject to amendment, depending on the outcome of a peace process and its successful implementation.

Just as the United States is poorly placed to broker a peace settlement, it will also require third-party assistance in overseeing the implementation of an accord, particularly one that calls for the withdrawal of American forces. The disarmament, demobilization, and reintegration of Afghan forces will be an essential element of any peace agreement. Given that there are between 25,000 and 35,000 insurgents but more than 250,000 Afghan army and police—a number far in excess of what the country will be able to afford or that donors will fund once the fighting ceases—the demobilization of government forces is likely to be even more demanding and certainly more expensive than the demobilization of the insurgents.[1] Indeed, some of the insurgents will probably have to be integrated into the government forces even as the total number of government forces is brought down. This will make it all the more important that those being marshaled out receive generous severance packages and some prospect of subsequent employment.

Of course, the United States will want to phase the implementation of any accord so that the removal of American forces occurs at the end of the process, by which time much of this local demobilization should be in train. The United States will also, as will be appropriate, insist that, before a full American departure, the Taliban completely break with Al Qaeda and other terrorist networks, evidence of which will be both (1) the Taliban's surrender of all its non-Afghan terrorist leaders still enjoying its hospitality and (2) its agreement to suitable means of verifying that these leaders are not invited back.

Even assuming such sequencing, the implementation of a peace accord will require a level of mutual trust likely to be absent on both sides. Additionally, whenever American and NATO troops do ultimately depart, they will leave behind something of a power vacuum. It will be important, therefore, to identify during the negotiating pro-

---

[1] Number of insurgents according to an Afghan Defense Ministry spokesman ("Up to 35,000 Insurgents Active in Afghanistan: Official," *Peoples Daily Online*, February 9, 2011); number of Afghan army and police according to a NATO news release (North Atlantic Treaty Organization, "Afghan National Security Forces (ANSF)," media backgrounder, March 2011).

cess some follow-on international presence, military as well as political, that can oversee the process of implementation. This presence need not be powerful enough to compel adherence (something even the United States and NATO have not been strong enough to do), but it should be sufficiently robust to deal with marginal spoilers and to set a high threshold for evasion by any party of its undertakings. This is a role that United Nations peacekeeping forces have successfully played in many other such circumstances, so that organization is the logical candidate to deploy a post–peace agreement force into Afghanistan.

Iraq is an inexact parallel to Afghanistan, but several components of any peaceful solution in the latter are likely to be similar to those employed in the former. First, the United States will have to tolerate—indeed, seek to broker—the inclusion of former insurgents in an enlarged coalition government. Second, the United States will have to promise to "go home," withdrawing its remaining combat forces on a fixed, mutually agreed schedule. Third, Washington will need to remain heavily engaged in the implementation of whatever accord is reached.

We thus recommend that the United States seek the appointment of a United Nations–endorsed facilitator to promote agreement among all the necessary parties to an Afghan peace process regarding a venue, participation, and the agenda for talks. We believe that Germany (perhaps Bonn) might be a good locale for such talks, as might a site in Turkey. Alternatively, if the Taliban objects to a NATO locale, Geneva is a neutral site where the parties could conveniently converge. Doha, where exploratory talks are reportedly under way between American and Taliban representatives under the auspices of German and Qatari officials, is another viable locale. We recommend that only the Afghan parties take formal part in the core negotiations over their country's future but that all of the major external stakeholders, including India, Iran, Pakistan, Russia, and the United States, conduct parallel, less formal discussions with a view to exercising convergent influence on the Afghan parties.

This will not be easy, given the divergent interests and objectives of the various actors. Figure S.1 illustrates the views of the main stakeholders on the issues likely to be at the center of any Afghan peace process. It distinguishes among nine external actors and the following three Afghan parties: the Kabul government, the Taliban, and the legal opposition to the Karzai government (which includes elements of the former Northern Alliance and of current civil society). We believe that this third group will ultimately have to be dealt with outside the formal negotiating process or included in it via incorporation within the Afghan government delegation; one way or another, its concerns will also need to be addressed.

The issues are withdrawal of NATO forces, the residual commitments and arrangements to combat terrorism, a commitment by the Afghan parties not to allow their territory to be used against any third party (nonalignment), the reciprocal commitment by Afghanistan's neighbors not to allow their territories to be used to destabilize Afghanistan (noninterference), a promise of continuing American security assistance, a United Nations peacekeeping operation, a commitment by Afghanistan and its neighbors to cooperate against drug trafficking, arrangements for power sharing among the Afghan factions, the role of Islam and sharia law, and commitments by the international community to continue economic assistance to Afghanistan.

Figure S.1
Stakeholder Views About Issues Central to the Peace Process

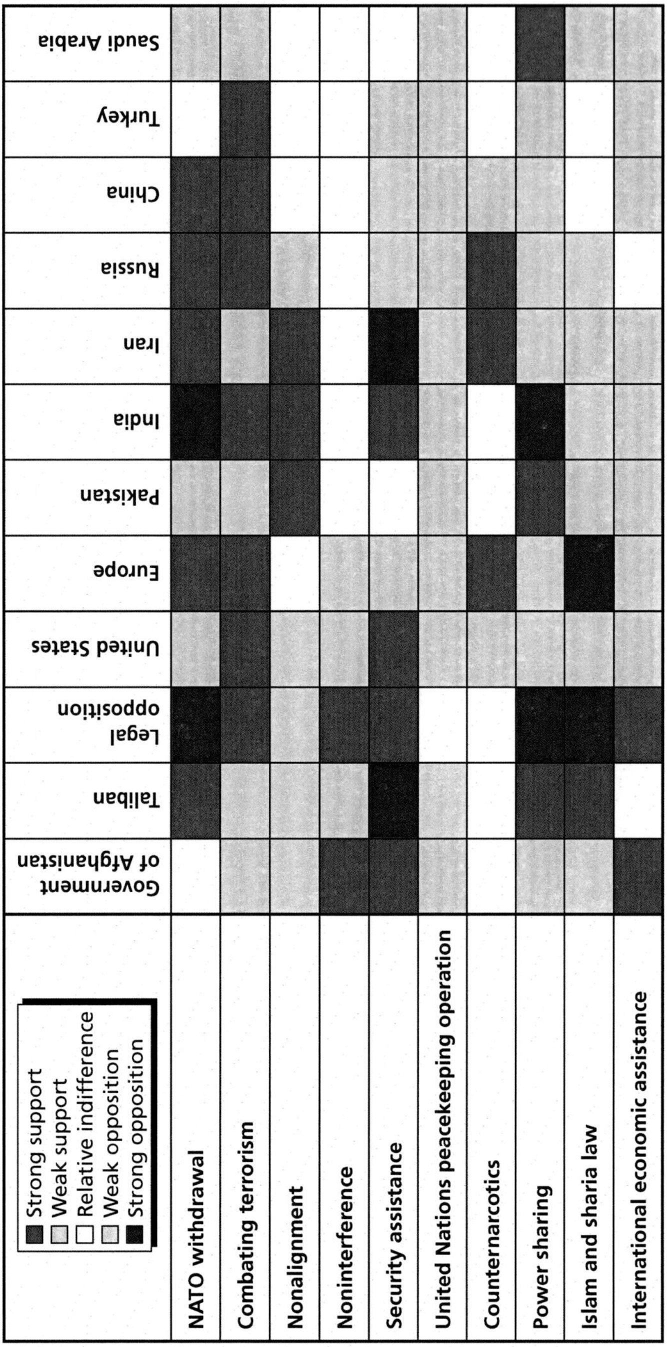

Legend:
- ■ Strong support
- ▨ Weak support
- □ Relative indifference
- ▤ Weak opposition
- ■ Strong opposition

Stakeholders (columns): Government of Afghanistan, Taliban, Legal opposition, United States, Europe, Pakistan, India, Iran, Russia, China, Turkey, Saudi Arabia

Issues (rows):
- NATO withdrawal
- Combating terrorism
- Nonalignment
- Noninterference
- Security assistance
- United Nations peacekeeping operation
- Counternarcotics
- Power sharing
- Islam and sharia law
- International economic assistance

Acknowledgments

We would like express appreciation to Jeff Laurenti and The Century Foundation for organizing the consultations upon which much of this work is based. We thank Lakhdar Brahimi and Thomas Pickering for heading those talks, and we thank the other task force participants, from whom we learned much: Barbara K. Bodine, Hikmet Çetin, Steve Coll, Robert Finn, Jean-Marie Guéhenno, Igor Sergeyevich Ivanov, Walter Kolbow, Lawrence J. Korb, Sadako Ogata, Francesc Vendrell, and Wang Yingfan. We are grateful to four outside readers who gave the draft a close critical read: Jean-Marie Guéhenno, Michael Wahid Hanna, Seth Jones, and Michael Semple. We appreciate the insights, provided through conversations or their own writings, offered by Aisha Ahmad, Milton Bearden, Stephen Biddle, Tina Bloem, Eliot Cohen, Wolfgang Danspeckgruber, Asad Durrani, Christine Fair, Robert Finn, Tom Freston, David Gordon, Antonio Giustozzi, Antje Grawe, Imtiaz Gul, Robert Hutchings, Minna Järvenpää, Felix Kuhn, Peter Lavoy, Madeline LePage, MaryBeth Long, Daniel Markey, Tug McGraw, Ishaq Naderi, Joanna Nathan, John Nicholson, Mitchell Reiss, Mitchell Shivers, Martin Smith, Marin Strmecki, Dmitri Trenin, Alex Strick van Linschoten, Martine von Bijier, Matthew Waldman, Michael Waltz, and Bobby Wilkes.

We are also indebted for their insights to the many American, European, Indian, Pakistani, and Russian officials to whom we spoke and to a number of serving and former members of the Government of Afghanistan and the Taliban insurgency. We alone are solely responsible for the contents of this monograph, whose conclusions represent our personal views and not necessarily those of any of our interlocutors.

Abbreviations

DDR	disarmament, demobilization, and reintegration
FATA	Federally Administered Tribal Areas
HiG	Haqqani and Hekmatyar
IEA	Islamic Emirate of Afghanistan
IRGC	Islamic Revolutionary Guard Corps
ISAF	International Security Assistance Force
ISI	Directorate for Inter-Services Intelligence
NATO	North Atlantic Treaty Organization
NGO	nongovernmental organization
TTP	Tehrik-e-Taliban Pakistan
UN	United Nations

CHAPTER ONE

Introduction

A number of recent studies have made the case for a negotiated peace in Afghanistan.[1] Both of us participated in one such inquiry, conducted under the auspices of The Century Foundation, whose results were published in March 2011.[2] In the course of that effort, we joined with a number of other American and international experts in visiting Kabul, Islamabad, and several other relevant capitals to hear firsthand from various potential participants in an Afghan peace process how they viewed the prospects, objectives, and possible outcomes. That study concluded that there was a sufficient confluence of interest on the part of the major parties to the war in Afghanistan to make a negotiated settlement feasible and worth pursuing. The Afghan government and, more recently, American officials have come to a similar conclusion.[3]

This monograph focuses somewhat less on whether and more on how a peace process for Afghanistan could be organized. We begin by

---

[1]   See, for example, The Century Foundation International Task Force on Afghanistan in Its Regional and Multilateral Dimensions, *Afghanistan, Negotiating Peace*, Washington, D.C.: 2011; Minna Järvenpää, *Making Peace in Afghanistan: The Missing Political Strategy*, Washington, D.C.: United States Institute of Peace, Special Report No. 267, 2011; Thomas Ruttig, *The Battle for Afghanistan: Negotiations with the Taliban*, Washington, D.C.: New America Foundation, May 23, 2011; Michael Semple, *Reconciliation in Afghanistan*, Washington, D.C.: United States Institute of Peace, 2009; and Matt Waldman, *Dangerous Liaisons with the Afghan Taliban: The Feasibility and Risks of Negotiations*, Washington, D.C.: United States Institute of Peace, Special Report No. 256, 2010.

[2]   The Century Foundation, 2011.

[3]   In a February 18, 2011, speech to the Asia Society, Secretary of State Hillary Clinton extended an explicit and unpreconditioned offer to negotiate a peace settlement in Afghanistan.

closely examining the political and military context in which negotiations could take place. We then review the interests and attitudes of each of the possible parties to a peace process, including the two main Afghan protagonists and the most interested external actors. Next, we set out a possible path from talks about talks to actual negotiations to implementation of an agreement. We then lay out the likely terms of any resultant accord and conclude with recommendations for American policy.

Throughout the monograph, our assessments of the various stakeholders' interests and objectives are based largely on our prior experience in dealing with these governments over the years and on recent conversations with active and former officials, representatives, and expert observers affiliated with each of the actors. Unless otherwise noted, our assessments should be considered the product of our experience and conversations.

Both authors have worked on Afghanistan in the past, one as the George W. Bush administration's first special envoy to that country in the aftermath of the attacks of September 11, 2011, and the other as an assistant secretary of defense responsible for this theater of war during the second term of that administration. We are thus very mindful that any negotiating strategy must consider practical decisionmaking constraints, shifting objectives, and disagreements internal to each of the parties (and between them), as well as dissimulation, duplicity, and efforts by spoilers to derail a peace process.

As former practitioners, we recognize that Afghanistan is not the only "game in town" for most of the outside parties involved and that apparently unrelated considerations or random events will sometimes shape these parties' policies toward a peace accord. As the monograph makes clear, we are quite aware of the many obstacles to an agreement, and we believe the process will probably require years of talking. During this time, fighting will likely continue and may even intensify. Negotiation does not represent an easy or early path out of Afghanistan for the United States and its North Atlantic Treaty Organization allies, but it is the only way in which this war is likely to end in a long-term peace.

CHAPTER TWO

Ambivalence, Convergence, and Negotiation

The paramount American objective in Afghanistan should be to prevent that country from again becoming a host to, and its government from becoming a willing ally of, Al Qaeda. The existence of other terrorist havens—in Pakistan, Somalia, and Yemen—has led many Americans to question what seems to be a disproportionately heavy investment in Afghanistan. Yet, in none of these other places is there a partnership between the local governments and Al Qaeda such as existed between that organization and the Taliban regime prior to the attacks of September 11, 2011. Operating more or less openly within a friendly state, as Al Qaeda did in pre-9/11 Afghanistan, gives a terrorist group far more leeway in planning, organizing, financing, and directing terrorist attacks than is the case when the organization is forced to conduct its activities covertly within a hostile state, such as Pakistan or Yemen, or even one with no government at all, such as Somalia. American forces went into Afghanistan in 2001 to break up the partnership between Al Qaeda and the government of Afghanistan. Preventing the return of an Al Qaeda–backed government in Kabul is the bottom-line reason why American and North Atlantic Treaty Organization (NATO) forces remain there today.

The current American military and monetary commitment to Afghanistan largely guarantees that terrorist attacks against the American homeland will not be mounted from that country. The price for this assurance is high, however. As time passes and the memory of the 9/11 attacks fades, as other Al Qaeda sites (such as Yemen) appear more threatening, and as no further large-scale terrorist incidents take place in the United States, Americans are becoming increasingly desirous of reducing this burden. As a result, maintaining anything like current troop and economic assistance levels in Afghanistan appears to be politically unsustainable for more than a few more years.

Some have argued that the United States should shift from counterinsurgency to a counterterrorism-focused effort, one that relies on drone strikes and night raids by special operations forces to prevent the return of Al Qaeda. But such a strategy is viable only as long as the United States can base these assets, along with the associated intelligence collection capabilities, somewhere in Afghanistan. This would clearly not be possible if the Taliban returned to power and, with Al Qaeda backing, secured control of most of the country. So, advocating an American shift toward counterterrorism is simply another way of urging the transfer of counterinsurgency responsibilities to the Afghan army and police.

The United States and its partners thus have two possible strategies. One is to build up an indigenous Afghan capacity to secure and govern the country and block the return of a fundamentalist regime with terrorist ties. The other, not necessarily inconsistent, course of action is to help broker a peace accord that ends the war on terms that also block the access of foreign terrorist organizations to Afghan real estate. Shifting the military burden to Afghan forces in this manner can only go so far. Afghanistan is too poor, undeveloped, and internally divided to be able secure its territory and protect its population without both help from the larger international community and the active cooperation of its neighbors. As long as Pakistan permits and indeed supports an insurgency intent on overthrowing the government in Kabul, no amount of training, mentoring, and equipping Afghan armed forces will allow these units to fully replace the American and NATO forces currently on the ground. Nor would Afghanistan ever be in a position to pay for the kind of security forces needed to replace, even partially, departing American and NATO troops.

It is also true, however, that there is no hope for an acceptable negotiated peace unless the insurgent Taliban leadership faces the prospect of at least an enduring military stalemate, if not outright defeat. This means that the military requirements for a negotiated outcome

are the same as those for the "Afghanization" option. Only a negotiated settlement offers the possibility, however, of achieving the United
States' preeminent objective, ending the war, and allowing a very large
reduction in the scale of the American commitment. The strongest
argument for negotiations is that they are not an alternative to war but
a complement to it, just as military operations are an indispensable element of peace negotiations.

Afghan Attitudes

There is strong support throughout Afghan society for a negotiated
peace. This sentiment is particularly strong within the Pashtun population, but it is also the majority view among other ethnic groups.
President Hamid Karzai and his inner circle are also motivated to seek
a peace agreement by the continually growing levels of violence; their
perception of waning support from Western allies; their fear of being
"sold out" by a separate peace negotiation between the Americans, the
Pakistanis, and elements of the Taliban under Pakistani control; and
their calculation that the Kabul government may be able to negotiate directly with Islamabad a broad-based arrangement that will put
enough pressure on the Taliban to bring the Taliban to the table. President Karzai and his advisers also believe that they can bring enough of
the leadership of the former Northern Alliance into a peace process—
through Peace Jirgas and Peace Councils—to make such a deal stick.

   Whether the insurgent leadership is interested in negotiations is
uncertain. Central Intelligence Agency Director Leon Panetta, in congressional testimony, has stated,

> We have seen no evidence that they [the insurgent leaders] are
> truly interested in reconciliation, where they would surrender
> their arms, where they would denounce al-Qaeda, where they
> would really try to become part of that society. We've seen no
> evidence of that and very frankly, my view is that with regards
> to reconciliation, unless they're convinced the United States is
> going to win and that they're going to be defeated, I think it's

very difficult to proceed with a reconciliation that's going to be meaningful.[1]

Interestingly, President Barack Obama, speaking later the very same day, took a less dismissive view of reconciliation, stating,

> I think that we have to view these efforts with skepticism, but also openness. The Taliban is a blend of hard-core ideologues, tribal leaders, kids that basically sign up because it's the best job available to them. Not all of them are going to be thinking the same way about the Afghan government, about the future of Afghanistan. And so we're going to have to sort through how these talks take place.

He went on to characterize Pakistani efforts to broker talks as "a useful step."[2]

There appear to be both much talking across the lines and repeated references in the media to initial official and unofficial contacts between figures representing Washington and figures purporting to represent the Taliban. Such regional experts as Ahmed Rashid, Barnett Rubin, and Michael Semple believe that the Taliban leadership is interested in negotiations and could be profitably engaged in such a process. This view is buttressed by conversations, in which we participated, with a number of midranking current Taliban political and military figures and with former senior Taliban leaders.

More recently, American officials have engaged in similarly exploratory but more official discussions with Taliban intermediaries. Clearly, thus, some elements of the insurgency are at least seriously interested in talking about negotiations, even if they may not yet be ready to fully engage in such a process. Elements within the Taliban and its associated components, including some in the Haqqani and Hekmatyar (HiG) networks, appear to be tiring of decades of war and

---

[1] Scott Shane, "Pakistan's Push on Afghan Peace Leaves U.S. Wary," *New York Times*, June 28, 2010.

[2] The White House, Office of the Press Secretary, "Remarks by President Obama at G-20 Press Conference in Toronto, Canada," June 27, 2010.

ready to negotiate, although others claim to believe that the insurgents can sustain the conflict indefinitely and that NATO's commitment to the war and to the Karzai government is wavering.

The recent death of Osama Bin Laden may help motivate Taliban leaders in two respects: first, making them more anxious about their own security and, second, perhaps removing whatever personal link there may have been between those leaders and Bin Laden. The latter may make it easier for the Taliban leaders to cut their remaining ties to Al Qaeda, a key American and NATO demand. The leadership of the Taliban's Quetta Shura has several incentives to negotiate, including

- the fact that many of its leaders have been killed by American special operations forces inside Afghanistan and by Central Intelligence Agency drone strikes in Pakistan
- the gradual attenuation of the Quetta Shura's command over the Taliban organization as a result of this attrition
- fear that the United States may be preparing to stay indefinitely in the absence of an accord
- the perception that the United States and its NATO allies may, on the other hand, be ready to negotiate terms of exit rather than fight to the end
- anger over Pakistani manipulation and intimidation, combined with a fear of being sold out by Islamabad in a separate deal with Kabul and Washington.

Trust between the Quetta Shura and Islamabad, always in short supply, seems to have deteriorated further over the past year.

The Role of External Actors

Question a Bosniak, Croat, or Serb about the basis of their mutual antagonisms and one gets a historical narrative dating back a millennium or more. Conflicts between Kurds, Sunni, and Shia Arabs in Iraq have a similarly long history. Ask the same of a Hazara, Pashtun, Tajik, or Uzbek citizen of Afghanistan, however, and one finds that their ethnically based hostilities only seem to go back a few decades, anterior to which many of them recall, however erroneously, a golden era when everyone lived together in peace. Even today, despite the antagonisms bred of 30 years of civil war, Afghanistan's Uzbek population does not want to live in Uzbekistan, its Tajiks in Tajikistan, its Pashtuns in Pakistan, or its Hazara in Iran. Among Pashtuns, the major tensions are with each other and across tribal lines, not ethnic or linguistic fault lines. There is no ethnic cleansing under way in Afghanistan. The vast majority of Afghans accept that theirs is a multilingual, multi-ethnic country. At the same time, they all feel entitled to a greater share in its governance (and in the patronage that flows from it) than others are prepared to accord them. Theirs is thus a conflict over power sharing, not national identity, and is therefore, in principle, more susceptible to compromise.

Agreement between the main Afghan parties is a necessary but insufficient prerequisite for peace. Unlike Iraq and Yugoslavia, strong states divided by even stronger ethnic antipathies, Afghanistan is a weak polity that has been torn apart by its near and more-distant neighbors, not unlike the hapless sheep which is pulled apart by mounted riders in *buzkashi*, the Central Asian version of polo. Unless these parties are drawn into the process in some fashion, no peace accord will hold. And until these parties sense that there is a credible endgame for forging a peace accord in Afghanistan that protects their vital interests, and until they gain some clarity into both the process and terms of a negotiated endgame, they have every incentive to continue to meddle destructively and promote the divisions between Afghans.

The Soviet invasion of Afghanistan was sparked by internal divisions among Afghan political factions after that "golden era" of unity and independence was rudely terminated by a coup and countercoup led by competing factions of leftist modernizing elites in Kabul. These divisions were fanned into a much larger and more enduring conflict with the involvement of the Pakistan, Saudi Arabia, and the United States. After the 1989 withdrawal of Soviet troops and the subsequent withdrawal of American assistance, India, Iran, and eventually Russia stepped in to limit Pakistani influence. Only in the aftermath of 9/11 was the United States briefly able to engineer a reconfiguration of these external players toward a common purpose: the overthrow of the Taliban and its replacement by the current regime.

This convergence of interests proved short-lived. Despite intense American prodding and massive American aid, Pakistan continues to allow the Afghan Taliban almost unfettered access to its border regions while its officials complain bitterly about four Indian consulates in neighboring Afghanistan as "nests of spies." Iran has continued to support Karzai and his government, but it is also hedging its bet (and tweaking the United States) by providing limited material support to insurgent groups. American forces in Afghanistan have tried to reduce their reliance on lines of supply through Pakistan by increasing shipments through Central Asia, but it may be years before this route can replace reliance on Pakistan. These shipments raise Russian anxieties about encroachment on its own sphere of influence. China has announced plans for a large investment in mining Afghan copper but is otherwise the least engaged of the major powers, despite being the only one to actually border Afghanistan.

In the event of a pell-mell American and European retreat, these other states would likely revert to their historical patterns of behavior, arming and financing their proxies and thereby pulling Afghanistan asunder. The result would be a return to the earlier constellation of civil war, with India, Iran, and Russia supporting northern, non-Pashtun resistance to a Pakistan-backed Pashtun hegemony. If Afghan history is any guide, this conflict would be considerably more violent than the one currently under way, producing many more casualties, larger refugee flows, and expanded opportunities for violent extremist groups to use Afghan territory, as they already do Pakistan, as a hub for more-distant attacks. And Al Qaeda would make much of the propaganda coup of militant mujahidin driving a second Great Power from Afghanistan just two decades after the Red Army's humiliating retreat across the Amu Darya River.

Pakistan's Ambivalent Stance

Among these external players, Pakistan is universally recognized as the most pivotal. The Pakistani government—including the military and its Directorate for Inter-Services Intelligence (ISI)—has offered to help broker a peace agreement between Kabul and the Taliban. Some Pakistani leaders now perceive themselves as standing in the crosshairs of domestic Islamic extremists, principally those of the Tehrik-e-Taliban Pakistan (TTP, or Pakistani Taliban). They would find it easier to deal with the insurgency in the Federally Administered Tribal Areas (FATA), the Northwest Frontier Province, and Baluchistan if the Afghan front were closed off by a peace accord. Indeed, this prospect may have replaced the notion of "strategic depth" in Afghanistan (i.e., using Afghanistan both as a locale for recruiting and training anti-Indian terrorists and as a bulwark against India doing the obverse) in Pakistani military thinking. Nevertheless, suspicions of India's hostile intentions in Afghanistan will never be fully assuaged. The Pakistanis also perceive that a messy end to American involvement in Afghanistan—including the persistent narrative in Western media that the Taliban insurgency is really a cat's paw of the ISI (a perception inflamed by the WikiLeaks material)—would imperil long-term Western financial and military support for Pakistan. These at least are the explanations that Pakistani officials and commentators have offered for their government's recent interest in helping broker a peace accord that would afford the Taliban significant influence in a new Afghan government, particularly in the regions bordering Pakistan, commensurately reducing Indian influence there.

Given the sharp shift in Pakistani public opinion against domestic militants that is the result of recent bloodshed—violent intimidation, suicide bombings, and the indiscriminate murder of innocent civilians, in particular—Pakistani civilian politicians are prepared to stand behind the military in promoting peace negotiations. Nonetheless, the range of views toward Afghanistan inside the Pakistani national security establishment remains wide, and although the Pakistanis may be willing to facilitate a peace process—and agree to a number of undertakings—they are likely to retain to the end some of their links with the Afghan insurrection.

There is a parallel, darker narrative regarding Pakistani interests and intentions that bodes less well for a peace process and for Pakistan acting as a helpful partner in the search for peace in Afghanistan. Pakistan's military establishment may still believe that the Taliban is a manageable proxy that is quite separate from the internal threat of its own militants. It may still view events in Afghanistan entirely through the lens of Indian encirclement. It may fear that an end to the Afghan conflict will bring a sharp diminution in American aid to Pakistan. Finally, it may be convinced that it has enough sources of leverage over the Americans (including the vulnerable logistics supply lines used to conduct the Afghan war and the ISI's cooperation against Al Qaeda) that it can play a double game in Afghanistan indefinitely. Only time, and Pakistan's actions once a peace process begins, will tell.

Reintegration Versus Reconciliation

The United States under the George W. Bush administration was not, in principle, opposed to peace talks. Until recently, however, Washington has preferred to concentrate on detaching Taliban foot soldiers and lower-level field commanders from the fight, a process called *reintegration*, arguing that any top-down effort to engage the insurgency's higher leadership should await improvements on the battlefield.

The attractions of reintegration are evident. Each insurgent brought over weakens the enemy while it correspondingly strengthens the government forces. In Iraq, such a process helped break the back of the Sunni insurgency, resulting in the massive defection of enemy fighters, who, in 2007, switched more or less overnight from killing American soldiers to working for them. This shift was achieved without the American or Iraqi governments having to make any concessions affecting the nature of the Iraqi state or the constitutional order that the United States has helped establish there.

Reconciliation, in contrast, would launch a process of mutual accommodation among two competing Afghan leaderships with very different visions of the Afghan state, inevitably opening the prospect of substantive trades-offs that make both American officials and many Afghans uneasy, even apprehensive.

The Obama administration has nevertheless recently come to embrace the possibility of negotiation with the insurgency leadership without preconditions. There are several reasons for this apparent change of heart.

First, it has become clearer that the wholesale shift in loyalties seen among the Sunni insurgents in Iraq in 2007 will be hard to replicate in Afghanistan. By 2007, the Sunni minority had been brutally and decisively beaten by majority Shia militias. It was only after this defeat that the Sunni turned to American forces for protection. In contrast, the Taliban insurgency in Afghanistan is rooted not in one of the country's ethnic minorities but within its largest community. Furthermore, these Pashtun insurgents have, until relatively recently, not been losing their civil war, but winning it.

Second, in Iraq, Al Qaeda had, by 2007, made itself very unwelcome among its Sunni allies through its indiscriminate violence and abusive behavior. In Afghanistan, Al Qaeda is hardly present— comprising a few hundred individuals at most—and certainly poses no comparable threat to the insurgent leadership or the Pashtun way of life. The Taliban will not break with Al Qaeda out of fear and resentment, as did the Sunni insurgency, but it may be led to break with Al Qaeda out of self-interest. The death of Bin Laden might eventually facilitate this process.

The third reason for the administration's change of heart is that it has a more accurate perception of the Afghan state, such as it is. Tribal structures in Afghanistan have been weakened by 30 years of civil war, assassinations perpetrated by the Taliban, and the rise of other local power brokers (including warlords, radical mullahs, and narcotraffickers). These changes have made Afghan elders a less influential set of interlocutors for the United States than were the Iraqi Sunni sheiks, who proved able to bring almost all of their adherents over with them when they decided to switch sides against Al Qaeda. More broadly, the Americans have increasingly realized that the Afghan state is far weaker than the Iraqi state, and possibly even more corrupt, and that it will take many years to create a viable Afghan state with institutions and structures on a national basis. If the purpose of the American military surge into Afghanistan was to buy time to build up the indigenous armed forces, and if the purpose of these forces was to buy time until the Afghan state could be built into a legitimate entity, then the timeline for building up the Afghan state ultimately paces the process for victory in Afghanistan, and that point now appears to be very far out in the future.

Finally, American and NATO military power in Afghanistan is now at its apogee and about to begin a slow decline. President Obama has begun a drawdown of American forces and promised to have withdrawn entirely from combat there by 2014. Most other coalition partners will probably be gone well before then. The hope is that the Afghan army and police can fill in behind departing Western forces, but military pressure on the insurgency seems as likely to recede as advance in the future. In terms of negotiating from strength, therefore, the current military balance is probably as good as it is going to get.

Although reintegration and reconciliation are conceptually distinct, there is a potential synergy between the two efforts. To the extent that Kabul and Washington are known to be talking to the insurgent leadership about peace, NATO commanders in the field are likely to have more success engaging and co-opting local insurgent leaders. To the extent that local efforts are successful in peeling away lower-level commanders and their troops, the top leadership will come under more pressure to negotiate seriously while it still has leverage.

These considerations, along with the realization that the Pakistanis are not going to move against Afghan insurgent sanctuaries in Pakistan any time soon, led the Obama administration to give President Karzai a green light to pursue his efforts to engage the insurgent leadership. In doing so, the Obama administration has reaffirmed but subtly altered three redlines originally set by the George W. Bush administration. First, the insurgents should sever all ties with Al Qaeda. Second, they should agree to operate politically within the confines of the existing Afghan constitution. Third, they should lay down their arms. Until recently, American officials had left vague whether these three desiderata were preconditions to talks or negotiating objectives. In a February 18, 2011, speech to the Asia Society, Secretary of State Hillary Clinton clearly stated that they were the desired end point of negotiations, not the price of entry.

Prospects for and Obstacles to Agreement

From the standpoint of the various interested parties, some motives for favoring a negotiated solution may be short-lived, and others may wax and wane over the coming years. Some motives are mutually reinforcing, and others may and will work at cross-purposes. Overall, there appears to be a volatile combination of policy disagreement and sheer confusion about the prospects of a peace accord among nearly all the potential participants.

Powerful forces in Afghanistan, Iran, and Pakistan would prefer indefinite warfare to any peace settlement, not least because of the vast sums of American money being spent on both sides of the Durand Line. In Afghanistan, these potential spoilers include local contractors (particularly security contractors), corrupt officials, and drug dealers, all of whom would find it more difficult to prosper in a peacetime environment. Pakistan would also lose considerable revenue from American assistance and NATO transit traffic were the war to end. Although the Iranian leadership wants an eventual American withdrawal, keeping American troops tied down in Afghanistan serves its short-term interests.

A peace accord is only one of several possible end states for the current conflict. Other potential outcomes include (1) an inconclusive "war without end"; (2) a gradual extension of the Kabul government's control over more of the country, achieved by dividing and conquering elements of the insurgency through a skillful reintegration strategy but leaving large pockets of violent opposition and lawlessness; and (3) the victory of the Taliban insurgency, at least in the south and east. Such a Taliban victory would likely lead to the eventual collapse of the Kabul government and to renewed civil war along ethnic fault lines, perhaps resulting in de facto partition of Afghanistan.

For the next year or two, the situation on the ground in Afghanistan is likely to fall somewhere on the spectrum between (1) and (2), with security and governance varying in a district-by-district mosaic. As Western forces progressively withdraw, the prospects for the third outcome increase. The timing of a serious peace initiative will thus be critical. The longer negotiations are delayed, the less influence the United States is likely to have, and the more unsatisfactory it is likely to find the outcome.

CHAPTER THREE

The Actors

Any negotiator should begin by considering the views and perspectives of the other side: crudely put, what do they want and what do they fear? How is their policy decisionmaking process structured? Who negotiates, concurs in, or vetoes an accord? Looking forward along a likely timeline, what pressures, including political or military calendars, will likely shape their decisionmaking? Do they believe that time is on their side? As far as one can tell in advance, what are the likely "must haves" and what are merely the "want to haves"? Notably, what are the deal-breakers? Who do they think can ultimately deliver on the objectives that they really need? What are the likely sticking points once a negotiation is under way? From a practical standpoint, what incentives or threats could likely move them off these sticking points in the pursuit of a viable peace accord?

The overarching consideration in this assessment of the parties to any Afghan peace process is coherence. It matters a great deal to a negotiating strategy how efficient, unitary, or fractured is the decisionmaking of the participants, and how broad and deep is the consensus within a given government on policy goals in Afghanistan. This is similar but not identical to the strong state/weak state distinction often made by political scientists. The low level of coherence in most of the actors in an Afghan peace process will be a seriously complicating factor in orchestrating a positive outcome that meets American objectives.

For example, the Kabul government is both weak and incoherent; the Taliban, back when it was in power, was an even weaker state actor than the current government in Kabul. As a guerrilla insurgency in the field, the Taliban will be even more incoherent than Kabul with regard to the terms of ending the war, although we know little about where the lines of internal disagreement run inside the Quetta Shura. The military in Pakistan and the ayatollahs and Revolutionary Guard in Iran are capable of ruthless, focused pursuit of their respective goals in Afghanistan, even though their governments, on the whole, are incoherent and badly divided.

Low coherence is not good news for the prospects of an accord. Incoherent actors are difficult and unreliable counterparties in any negotiation. The actors may change course in midstream, their terms are likely to shift and be retraded, and their commitment to implementation is always suspect. For these reasons, an Afghan peace process will probably bear little resemblance to the Congress of Vienna, the Treaty of Versailles, or the Six Party Talks on Korea, all cases in which the participants had pretty clear ideas about their interests, objectives, and limitations. Instead, an Afghan peace process may have more in common with the messy 1995 Dayton Accords, in which the several parties to the war in Bosnia, some states and some not, had to be put under a good deal of external pressure to come to the table and then to reconcile their differences.

This chapter examines four categories of actors: first, the two main Afghan parties who must be at the core of any negotiation; next, the two external parties with the greatest influence over events in Afghanistan (Pakistan and the United States); then, the other regional governments with great stakes in and influence over the outcome of any negotiations; and, finally, the wider circle of states that can be expected to play some role in such a process, including, crucially, in the implementation of any accord.

The Core

The Taliban

The coherence of the Afghan Taliban insurgency (which styles itself the Islamic Emirate of Afghanistan, or IEA) can be assessed in two dimensions, horizontal and vertical. The horizontal dimension refers to agreement on objectives among the top leadership, first within the Quetta Shura and then between the Quetta Shura and its affiliated groups, including the HiG networks.[1] Also potentially influential could be the views of TTP, Al Qaeda, and other transnational jihadi networks (such as those of the Chechens and Uzbeks) with roots in the lawless border regions. The vertical divide is between the top Quetta Shura leadership, most of whom are in Pakistan, and the warfighters at the local level, principally the Taliban's shadow governors and district military commanders.

From the perspective of evaluating a peace accord, the Afghan Taliban is highly decentralized and relatively incoherent both horizontally *and* vertically. Beyond the differing objectives of the HiG networks, the lingering Kandahari-Paktiawal rivalry is one of the largest potential lines of cleavage within the Quetta Shura itself. There are many other potential fractures within the insurgency's "network of networks," particularly given the Taliban fighters' contending personal and regional loyalties to their local tribal and religious leadership. As an experienced Pakistani journalist with long contacts with the Afghan Taliban told us, "The Taliban will split among themselves as soon as there is a peace negotiation that involves some power sharing."

The Afghan Taliban is overseen by four regional shura, which are (or were) located in Quetta, Peshawar, Miramshah, and Gerdi Jangal (the Quetta Shura is first in primacy), and by three associated networks: the Haqqani, Hizb-i-Islami (led by Gulbuddin Hekmatyar), and Mansur networks. The latter three networks overlap to varying degrees with the regional shura. The Haqqani and Mansur networks are represented on the Quetta Shura, as is the head of the Peshawar Shura, Maulvi Abdul Kabir. The role of the TTP in internal Afghan insurgent debates is unclear. What is clear is that both the United States and Pakistan wish the Afghan and Pakistani Taliban could be separated and isolated. Al Qaeda has interpenetrated both the Afghan Taliban and Pakistani Taliban to some degree, but its numbers are small, its lever-

---

[1] The Taliban's top leadership may have quitted Quetta Shura and perhaps dispersed to several locations. We retain the term *Quetta Shura* here not as a geographical locator but as the commonly used appellation of the insurgency's top leadership council.

age is decreasing, and its control over decisions is probably very limited. It will, however, do its best to sabotage any negotiation.

The Taliban has established a shadow national organization corresponding to most of Afghanistan, although it is more prevalent in the south and southeast. The IEA did, after all, exercise nominal control over 95 percent of the territory of Afghanistan for several years. Many of the local leaders of this shadow organization have been killed or captured, and the pace of attrition increased in 2010 due to expanded drone targeting and special operations raids and to the troop surge in Helmand and Kandahar. This pressure has also kept many insurgent leaders penned up on the Pakistan side of the border, further reducing their direct control over field operations.

For this and other reasons, there appears to be a good deal of de facto decentralization to local front district and provincial commanders. At its root, the Taliban insurgency, to an even greater degree than the Kabul government, is an agglomeration of local patron-client networks, with district leaders commanding the allegiance of their soldiers through a combination of military skill, personal bravery, religious piety, ruthlessness, tribal connections, fundraising skills, and political guile. When a district commander is removed by force, the next commander steps up in a selection process that combines local fortitude with approval from the Taliban leadership abroad. These younger commanders are familiar with the Taliban only as an insurgent force, not with its years in office, and they may feel less committed to its aging leadership.

This is not a situation likely to produce a kinder and gentler cadre of leaders, nor one necessarily more attentive to orders from Quetta Shura or the ISI. One intelligence officer told us,

> As older commanders are killed or captured, their replacements are both crueler and more extremist. The Quetta Shura has some control over who replaces these commanders, but not completely. So they are both aware [of] and alarmed about the changing complexion of their commanders in the field.

We do not know how much command and control the Quetta Shura continues to exercise at the ground level, but we do believe that it has been attenuated over time. With 80 to 90 percent of Taliban fighters operating in or close to their own communities, there is a mosaic of contending loyalties on the ground, and the lines of cleavage will only be revealed and tested as the terms of a peace agreement are negotiated.

As Antonio Giustozzi cautions,

> The network-based character of the Taliban structure makes it all the more important for them to move cautiously with regard to negotiations; the leadership would not want the single networks or individual commanders to move towards talks in sparse order. The movement would then risk disintegrating. The leadership will also want to stress aspects of any settlement which would facilitate its tasks of keeping the Taliban together: . . . a financial settlement and the integration of the military force.[2]

The Quetta Shura has imposed stringent rules banning district commanders from engaging in freelance peace discussions. As one Taliban district commander complained, "The peacemakers among us are most in peril and at risk of being killed, while the warmakers and the most militant commanders feel safe." (One reason to pursue reconciliation with the top insurgency leadership is that it may make it somewhat easier to also engage lower-level figures and peel them off. This, of course, is one of the reasons the top leadership will be cautious about entering such a process.)

There appear to be a number of subcommittees of the Rahbari Shura—a dozen or more, although both function and membership are obscure. The serving heads of the political and military subcommittees would probably be closely involved in negotiations on an accord, even at the early stages, with other functional subcommittees—such as prisoner affairs and the religious council—engaged as necessary. In any case, Mullah Mohammed Omar will have the final say on the negotiating objectives and will choose who negotiates on the Taliban's behalf. However, he will receive advice and consent from his inner circle and from the members of the Quetta Shura, among whom he will, prob-

---

[2] Antonio Giustozzi, *Empires of Mud: Wars and Warlords in Afghanistan*, New York: C. Hurst & Co. Ltd, 2009, p. 12.

ably with some difficulty, have to forge a consensus. He appears to be the only individual with credible authority over all Afghan Taliban factions, none of which have challenged his leadership in more than two decades. Indeed, even though many Taliban fighters in the south represent a new generation of jihadis, they still hold Mullah Omar in respect, and no other old-guard Taliban leader currently has such broad influence.

Mullah Omar has both legitimacy among the Taliban and some coercive power, but he is constrained by the consensual nature of the Quetta Shura; the quasi-independence (and bloody-mindedness) of affiliated networks, such as the HiG; the decentralized nature of the insurgency itself, which has seen a new set of leaders emerge "on the ground" as many midlevel Taliban leaders have been killed or captured; and Pakistani influence. Mullah Omar himself may at some point in this conflict be removed by an act of God, Pakistan, or the United States, and his removal would make the already low coherence of the Taliban even shakier.

The Hekmatyar, Haqqani, and Mansur network leaders could play spoiler roles in any negotiation if they perceived that they were being excluded from the process or that their interests were being sacrificed. Spoiler groups from among the local leadership of the Taliban at the district and provincial levels inside Afghanistan could also emerge to challenge an accord and to defy Mullah Omar's authority if an accord, in their view, seemed to have sold out the Taliban's core values or seemed in some way to threaten their local power base.

Finally, east of the Durand Line, the Pakistani Taliban could "declare war" on any accord that imposed terms that it considered threatening, as could Al Qaeda. Since the terms of any plausible peace accord would explicitly isolate both the TTP and Al Qaeda, a campaign of intimidation, kidnapping, and murder by these two groups targeting both the Kabul government *and* the Quetta Shura during the negotiation and implementation of a peace accord is virtually certain. This will raise the diplomatic and personal stakes for the negotiators in unpleasant ways.

Public opinion among a mostly illiterate rural population living in areas under partial or full Taliban control is shaped in large measure

by the ulema-led madrassas and mosques and by residual tribal structures. The Quetta Shura and other Taliban leaders have some capacity
to engage and shape the opinion of these ulema networks and residual
tribal structures. The religious leadership is likely to be sharply critical
of the terms of any accord that limits the role of sharia and protects
gender rights, but tribal leaders are more likely to focus on the economic, security, and governance terms of an accord.

We do not know how optimistic the Taliban leaders are about
their prospects in the war. President Obama's initial plan to begin
troop withdrawal in July 2011 apparently strengthened insurgent optimism that time was indeed on their side. Further public statements
by various American and NATO officials promising to hand over all
security responsibilities to the Kabul government by 2014 stretched
out this timetable but still encouraged the view that NATO could be
waited out. More-recent discussions between Washington and Kabul
about an enduring American-Afghan "strategic relationship" may be
dampening this optimism.

Despite severe setbacks on the battlefield over the past year, sec-
ondhand feedback through media reports and the Taliban's own propaganda nevertheless suggests a certain beleaguered optimism on the
part of the organization that it can wait out the United States and
its NATO allies, that the Europeans are already in retreat, and that
the Americans are searching for the exit as well. Our discussions with
current and former Taliban leaders, including several district military
and political commanders, tend to support this view, although the fact
that these figures would even meet with Western experts to discuss
the terms of a possible accord suggests that at least some midranking
Taliban figures have an open mind. Some maintained that they had
no alternative to fighting after having been frozen out of influence and
standing in their local communities. There is probably a multiplicity of
views among senior leaders and district commanders about whose side
time is on.

The Taliban leadership will have a long list of objectives in any
peace accord, as might be expected from a group that at one time ruled
most of the country and has been fighting a sustained war for nearly a
decade to regain that position. We know neither how much consistency

there is regarding the priority of these objectives within the insurgency leadership, either horizontally or vertically, nor which objectives are "hard" and which ones might be compromised on or traded off against other goals.

As noted earlier, the Taliban's primary objectives are, roughly in this order,

- the removal of foreign forces from Afghanistan, with no residual foreign military presence other than as part of temporary peace-keeping forces
- security for insurgents, particularly in the country's south and southeast, while neutralizing the military threat to the Taliban posed by the International Security Assistance Force (ISAF), the Afghan National Army, the Afghan National Police, and the Afghan National Security Directorate. This includes ending the targeting of the leaders and their families in Afghanistan and, importantly, in Pakistan as well.
- having the Taliban be recognized by the outside world as a legitimate political actor in Afghanistan, having key IEA leaders removed from the United Nations (UN) list of terrorists, and gaining the release of Taliban prisoners held in Pol-e-Charki, Guantanamo, and elsewhere
- establishing an extreme version of Islamic law throughout Afghanistan
- purging "corrupt" elements from Afghanistan, including local commanders and several figures who are part of the current government, and prosecuting or exiling some of the most violent warlords (as defined by the Taliban).

The first three of these objectives are likely "must haves" from the standpoint of the Taliban, although their timing is probably negotiable, since none of them can be achieved instantaneously. Some further institutionalization of Islamic law will probably also be considered essential by the Taliban leadership, although how much seems open to negotiation.

The Taliban leaders believe that only the United States can credibly deliver on the first objective and that Washington plays a key role in the second and third objectives as well. They do not believe that President Karzai on his own can credibly commit to these points, and therefore they appear relatively uninterested in talking to Kabul about them.

As a Taliban district commander told us, "The big question mark for us is whether the United States really intends to withdraw its forces from Afghanistan at some point, or whether they intend to maintain a long term strategic presence of their troops in Central Asia, as part of some American new world order." This skepticism was echoed by a Taliban district political leader from the south: "We do not believe the United States is serious about peace negotiations, otherwise why this big surge of troops? How can the United States really intend to leave Afghanistan if they are still building these huge bases, including the expanding airbase at Kandahar?"

The Quetta Shura also must recognize that Pakistan's cooperation is key to achieving the first two objectives, at least initially, and that, once they are achieved, Pakistan's leverage over the Taliban will decrease. Thus, as a peace accord unfolds, there will be intense negotiations between different elements of the Quetta Shura, HiG, and the Haqqani groups on one hand and the Pakistani government on the other. As we note elsewhere, there is deep and abiding distrust between the Taliban and Pakistan. As a former Taliban leader told us, "Pakistan will claim to you that they control us, but it is not so. The Pakistanis are liars and not trustworthy as intermediaries. They have our families in Pakistan as hostages and have hundreds of our people in jail." And as a regional expert with close contact with Taliban figures said, "Once they are convinced there is a serious peace process, the Taliban may use it to escape from being proxies. This gives the Taliban rather more incentive to behave well in a settlement than is generally anticipated."

When Taliban members speak publicly and privately about making Afghanistan an Islamic state, they are usually speaking about much more than jurisprudence. According to Matthew Waldman, "for the majority of insurgents interviewed, the concept of sharia as an objective was panoptic and multidimensional—not only religious and legal, but also political, moral, and cultural."[3] This implies some roll-back of gender and religious minority rights and an unspecified invo-cation of Islam in counternarcotics operations and law enforcement.

That said, there is likely to be some shifting priority among these objectives over time, and there are likely to be several points on which compromise is possible, probably with considerable variation horizon-tally and vertically. Subtle changes in the Taliban's public statements over time (including Mullah Omar's Eid proclamations), anecdotal evidence from experts in the field, and our conversations with Taliban figures suggest that these possible areas of compromise include

- severing ties with Al Qaeda and other extremist jihadi groups. However, as former Taliban foreign minister Mullah Wakil Muttawakil observed, "The longer this war goes on, the closer our links with Al Qaeda."
- some limited gender rights. The Taliban leadership has at times said that it will accept education for girls, and it has, in practice, sometimes allowed girls' schools to operate in some areas under its control.
- relaxing the imposition of some Wahhabi-style Islamic cultural rules (such as banning music and kite-flying) and some Sunni-centric legal rules, particularly in non-Pashtun areas and among Shia communities
- political accommodations and assurances for former Northern Alliance and non-Pashtun groups, based on some sort of decen-tralized structure or parliamentary system. This could be negoti-ated at the top or at the bottom. Such arrangements are likely to be more durable if they are negotiated at the district level "on the ground."
- sharing leadership. Mullah Omar may not necessarily be inter-ested in running Afghanistan again as its supreme leader, although he probably wants to influence or reform the consti-tutional structure. In the long run, if he is granted some kind of credible immunity by a government of national reconciliation and

---

[3] Waldman, 2010, p. 5.

is explicitly removed from American target lists and UN sanctions lists, Mullah Omar may prefer to return to his madrassa in Kandahar. On the other hand, if these conditions prove hard to obtain and harder to verify, he might prefer a residing in peaceful villa in Riyadh or Mecca to living in peril in Kandahar.

Giustozzi maintains that the Taliban "do not appear likely to accept the Afghan constitution even in a revised form; certainly they would demand a greater role for Islamic law in the legislation and a consequent Islamisation of the judiciary."[4] In terms of power sharing, Afghan government officials have been hinting that President Karzai is ready to offer a number of governorships and ministerial positions to Taliban members in the event of reconciliation, but the Taliban does not seem to be interested in joining President Karzai's system. In the existing presidential system, President Karzai could undo any appointment as he wishes, offering no guarantee to the Taliban that a deal would be respected in the medium or long term.

A financial package might also emerge as an essential complement to a political settlement, particularly if the Taliban has to renounce at least some of the revenue it currently gathers. The Taliban leadership would insist on a financial scheme benefiting the movement as a whole, rather than one consisting solely of individual incentives.[5]

In sum, we do not know whether the Taliban (at all levels) believes that time is on its side. We also do not know how coherent the insurgency is, either horizontally or vertically, with regard to negotiating a peace accord, although we believe it to be fairly incoherent across both dimensions, which is not necessarily good news. As in the case with Pakistan's ambivalent approach to a peace accord, we may not know the answer to either question until negotiations are under way.

The Kabul Government

The Kabul government is fragile, relatively new, and governing a very poor, war-torn country. Its uneasy relations with its neighbors and for-

---

[4] Giustozzi, 2009, pp. 24–25.

[5] Giustozzi, 2009, p. 12.

eign patrons alike constitute a congeries of overlapping patron-client networks in uneasy coalition rather than a modern nation-state's set of established foreign relations. This makes the Kabul government both a difficult partner in counterinsurgency operations and frustratingly incoherent with regard to a peace process.

Nevertheless, it is important not to overstate the inefficacy of the Kabul regime, particularly as seen from an Afghan perspective. In Western opinion, the war is going badly, and President Karzai appears to be illegitimate, inept, and corrupt. However, even given the difficulties of conducting accurate opinion polling in a war-torn country, multiple surveys suggest that the Afghan public has a very different view. In the most recent national poll, 59 percent of Afghans said that they think their country is moving in the right direction; just 28 percent of Americans feel the same about the United States.[6] Asked President Ronald Reagan's classic question—Are you better off today than five years ago?—63 percent of Afghans say "yes." President Karzai's government enjoys a 62 percent approval rating, and he personally is viewed positively by 82 percent of his compatriots. Afghan support for the presence of American forces fell between the end of 2009 and the end of 2010, but is still at 62 percent, much higher than the 39 percent of Americans who supported this same troop commitment in June of 2011.[7] Eight in ten Afghans express confidence in the Afghan National Army, and only a slightly lower number express confidence in their national police force. The Taliban, in contrast, is viewed unfavorably by nine in ten Afghans.[8]

It is not difficult to explain Afghan optimism. Since 2001, the country's gross domestic product has tripled. Ten years ago, there were fewer than 1 million children in school—almost all boys. In fall 2011, more than 8 million children will attend school—one-third of them

---

[6]   CBS News/New York Times Poll, June 2011. Retrieved from the iPOLL Databank, The Roper Center for Public Opinion Research, University of Connecticut, on July 7, 2011.

[7]   Pew Research Center for the People, June 2011. Retrieved from the iPOLL Databank, The Roper Center for Public Opinion Research, University of Connecticut, on July 7, 2011.

[8]   Gary Langer, "Afghanistan Poll: Where Things Stand 2010," ABCNews.com, November 30, 2010.

girls. Afghanistan's literacy rate will triple over the next decade as these children complete their education. Today, 80 percent of Afghans have access to basic health care facilities, almost twice as many as in 2005. Infant mortality has dropped by one-third, and adult longevity is going up. Perhaps most remarkably, half of all Afghan families now have telephones.[9]

Afghans are very concerned about still-rising violence, but this too needs to be seen in some context. The UN announced that, in 2010, more than 2,700 Afghan civilians were killed by insurgent, Afghan national, or NATO forces, the vast majority (75 percent) by antigovernment elements.[10] What is an annual figure for Afghanistan would have been a typical month in Iraq, a smaller country, back in the awful days of 2006. It represents a much smaller proportion of the population than does the murder rate in many American cities. Perhaps most importantly, from an Afghan perspective, it does not compare with the much higher levels of violence Afghans experienced in the 1980s and 1990s, when war with the Russians and then among Afghans themselves drove millions of citizens out of the country. Today's refugee flows, in contrast, are still on balance directed back into the country from both Pakistan and Iran.

Although polling data offer a better guide to Afghan opinion than mere anecdote, it is true that wide disparity exists in the distribution of social and economic advances, that the perception of corruption is widespread and a source of great resentment, and that significant disaffection remains in the areas of the country where the insurgency is most active. These areas have seen the least social and economic progress because they are in revolt, and they are in revolt in part because they have seen so little benefit from the new dispensation in Kabul.

Polling also reveals very strong support throughout the Afghan population for peace negotiations. Seventy-three percent of the

---

[9] Paul Miller, "Finish the Job: How the War Can Still Be Won," *Foreign Affairs*, January/February 2011, pp. 56–57.

[10] United Nations Assistance Mission in Afghanistan and Afghanistan Independent Human Rights Commission, *Afghanistan Annual Report 2010: Protection of Civilians in Armed Conflict*, Kabul, March 2011, p. x.

Afghan population favors negotiations between the Afghan national government and the Taliban, should the latter agree to stop fighting.[11] Afghans value what has been achieved over the past decade and have no intention of giving it up to return to life under the IEA, but they also regard the Taliban as an inescapable and not necessarily illegitimate part of the national fabric and one that should be brought back into the fold, although not at any cost.

These positive views of a peace process are not fully shared by those who might have the most to lose in such an accommodation, including elements of the old Northern Alliance leadership and much of civil society, particularly women's representatives. President Karzai knows he must reach out to his (nonviolent) political opposition, including former Northern Alliance factions, and negotiate with them over his shoulder as he hammers out the terms of a possible deal with the Taliban across a table. He has historically exhibited considerable skill and finesse in consensus-making, allocation of patronage, and finely tuned log-rolling, which has allowed him to build up his power from an originally very narrow base and to make the best of the weak hand he was dealt in 2002. These qualities could be quite useful if turned to the task of bringing former insurgent elements back into the political process. It remains to be seen whether he can sustain this adroit performance through a peace process. His initial steps—setting up a Peace Council with some civil society representation and appointing former Northern Alliance President Berhanuddin Rabbani to head it—suggest that he intends to maintain a careful balance, at least in the initial stages of any negotiation.

President Karzai, his family, and his inner circle of advisers will nonetheless remain the primary decisionmakers when it comes to the Kabul government's handling of any peace negotiations. The inner circle has taken on a more distinct Pashtun ethnic coloring since President Karzai's deliberate efforts to include more Hazara, Tajik, and other non-Pashtun ethnic groups in the run-up to the 2009 presidential election. Among the skeptics he must convince are former Northern Alliance leaders, politicians, and warlords. Some are currently

---

[11] Langer, 2010.

affiliated with the Karzai government; others, including former presidential candidates Younis Qanooni and Abdullah Abdullah, are in the "loyal" (i.e., legal) opposition. Although these figures disagree on many issues, they could, as a bloc, exercise a practical veto with respect to any accord. If they become too concerned about a re-Talibanized leadership emerging under some sort of reconciliation government, they could well take up arms in opposition to the accord.

President Karzai will continue to hold any real peace negotiations close to his vest, and he will continue to communicate with insurgent leaders via his family and other members of his trusted inner circle. One such trusted person is Mohammad Masoom Stanekzai, who heads the Afghan Peace and Reconciliation Program out of the Presidential Palace. Another is Foreign Minister Zalmai Rasool. President Karzai will keep a close hold on negotiations, chiefly through the offices of Engineer Mohammed Ibrahim Spinzada, President Karzai's deputy national security adviser and brother-in-law. As one European diplomat told us, perhaps with some exaggeration, "Engineer Spinzada has a black book with all the cell phone numbers of the Taliban leadership. He can talk to them any time and bring them in to Kabul to talk, and sometimes does."

Spinzada's preferred approach to peace negotiations appears to be to split off major elements of the insurgency, such as subnetworks of the Taliban or the Hekmatyar network, and focusing, group by group, on "reintegration" rather than an approach that would result in a political solution that involves true power sharing with the Taliban. As a senior Karzai government official told us, "Reconciliation does not mean that we are dealing with the Taliban as a political movement. If we can resolve the India issue with Pakistan, the Taliban will collapse."

President Karzai, on the other hand, would prefer to negotiate a deal with top insurgent leaders, although he appears to be open to working with midlevel figures as well, if the more senior figures will not make deals. He has been rebuffed on several occasions by figures at both levels. He and his inner circle continue to conduct parallel negotiations with the Pakistani military and political leadership, including Army Chief of Staff General Ashfaq Parvez Kayani; the general's ISI intelligence chief, Lieutenant-General Ahmad Shujah Pasha; and a cross-section of civilian politicians. In a set of multiday meetings in Kabul in mid-April 2011, Pakistani Prime Minister Yousaf Raza Gilani was the spokesman for a delegation that included Pakistan's top brass, notably Generals Kayani and Pasha. These talks seem to have been distinctly more positive in tone than President Karzai's previously testy meetings with a similar team led by then–President Pervez Musharraf. Abdul Hakim Mujahid, a member of President Karzai's Peace Council who had also served in the Taliban regime before its ouster, said of these talks, "Once we build trust between Pakistan and Afghanistan, that is the most important thing. Then negotiating with the Taliban is easy."[12]

Even as he talks to the Pakistanis over the heads of the Taliban leadership, President Karzai is nervous that American, European, or UN diplomats may conduct negotiations with the Taliban behind his back. He considers the British to be particularly untrustworthy in this regard, which helped account for his strong opposition to the appointment of Paddy Ashdown as head the UN Mission in Afghanistan in 2008 and for his doubts about former British ambassador to Afghanistan Sherard Cowper-Coles, who was outspoken about the need to negotiate with the Taliban. The Irish European Union staffer Michael Semple was expelled from Afghanistan for advocating (and conducting) "unauthorized" talks with the Taliban. Former Special Envoy Richard Holbrooke reportedly also antagonized President Karzai by making similar back-channel overtures to the insurgency.

Presumably, Afghanistan's parliament must approve the terms of an accord, but any deal will also be vetted informally with former Northern Alliance members of the Karzai government and perhaps with those in the "loyal" opposition. One of these senior opposition politicians told us that

> President Karzai's Peace Jirga in July [2010] socialized much of the Afghan government and public to a negotiated peace accord before the fact. Now, a Peace Council will be used by the Palace

---

[12] Alissa Rubin, "Afghan and Pakistani Leaders Meet in Peace Bid," *New York Times*, April 17, 2011, p. 8.

to sell the terms of any accord, if it is arrived at, after the fact. And so he will likely appoint Berhanuddin Rabbani or another senior former Northern Alliance figure to head up this Peace Council to make it more acceptable to the political opposition.

As predicted, former President Rabbani was subsequently appointed to this post.

Given how many powerful actors in the current government have a stake in continued conflict, foreign involvement, and the flow of international funds into Afghanistan, there are many who might act as spoilers in any peace process. For example, some members of President Karzai's family and inner circle see themselves with little or no future under an accord. If the insurgent leaders are granted significant power sharing in the south, which is a likely result, some of these influential figures could find themselves marginalized.

Several former warlords and local strongmen might fear becoming targets of prosecution or forced exile under the terms of an accord, and, unless guaranteed immunity or safe exile abroad, they too would become a roadblock to a settlement, or could even start another war. The Taliban will likely seek revenge on several former Northern Alliance military commanders, including Abdul Rashid Dostum, Mohammad Qasim Fahim, Ismail Khan, and Atta Mohamad Nur, at whose hands thousands of Taliban foot soldiers perished during the civil war and in the harsh military campaign of 2001–2002. These former Northern Alliance leaders have scores of their own to settle with the Taliban, originating in years of brutal oppression, terms in prison, and mass murder at the hands of Taliban forces when the Taliban swept into the north. Many senior officers of Hazara, Tajik, or Uzbek ethnic backgrounds in the Afghan National Army and the National Security Directorate (Afghanistan's main intelligence agency) have scores to settle too.

These antagonisms will probably cancel each other out in any peace negotiation, leaving little room, and perhaps none at all, for provisions relating to war crimes and so-called transitional justice. Instead, past crimes will more likely fester, overlaid on blood feuds and decades of double-dealing and treachery, under the façade of a government of national reconciliation. We understand the arguments for war crimes justice in democratic consolidation, but the context for negotiating a peace accord in Afghanistan is complex enough without re-injecting three decades of horror and revenge into the process.

Civil society groups, including those seeking to expand the role of women in government and the economy and those supporting human rights, free media, and opposing corruption, will also view any peace process very skeptically. These groups are heavily dependent on the international donor community and will likely seek to exert their influence primarily through that community. Civil society groups pose a challenge to the untrammeled exercise of authority (and self-dealing) by both the Karzai inner circle and Taliban members in forming a government of national reconciliation, and they will fear becoming the targets of state surveillance and selective violence.

President Karzai may be inclined to strike a top-level deal with the Taliban leaders and leaders of the former Northern Alliance groups, paying less attention to the interests of parties lower in the power hierarchy. Should this happen, less-important regional strongmen, elements within the military or intelligence services, and groups within civil society may morph into roadblocks or spoilers. On their own or allied with each other out of convenience, embattled warlords will appeal to their patrons abroad, and threatened civil society groups will almost certainly reach out to NATO governments, other donor countries (such as Japan), and Western civil society if they see their interests being compromised in a top-level deal. There will be a great deal of self-interested spin by many parties in Afghanistan as the peace process evolves.

The legions of security contractors employed by ISAF, diplomatic entities, businessmen, and nongovernmental organizations (NGOs) are a particularly potent group facing big losses if a peace accord is achieved. This contractor network overlaps with those of warlords, members of the government, local strongmen, elements of the Afghan army and police, the intelligence services, some in the Taliban, and many Pakistanis in complex ways. These elements have a lot of cash and weapons with which to cause trouble during the negotiation and implementation of any peace accord.

President Karzai would prefer that negotiations take place in Kabul. Kandahar might also be an option, although the security situation would make it less attractive. President Karzai would probably object to holding negotiations in Pakistan but might find acceptable a neutral site, such as Doha, Istanbul, or Geneva, or, perhaps to a lesser degree, Jakarta, Kuala Lumpur, or Riyadh.

President Karzai may not believe that time is on his side. His second and last term of office under the Afghan constitution ends in 2014, coincident with the scheduled completion of the withdrawal of American and European combat forces. There is some chance that President Karzai might attempt to use peace negotiations and an attendant constitutional revision to run for a third term. Alternatively, if Afghanistan were to move to a parliamentary system as a result of these negotiations (as many Afghans and Western observers think would better suit the country), there would be no legal obstacle to President Karzai seeking to become the Afghan Prime Minister.

President Karzai knows that support for him and his government is very low in many Western capitals. He feels that the European members of NATO have given up the military fight in Afghanistan, essentially handing it over to the Americans. He and his inner circle also have low and apparently declining trust in the reliability of the American commitment to Afghanistan. President Karzai is a close reader of American opinion polling and public comments made by American leaders about the war. He was deeply antagonized by Obama administration maneuvers to undercut him (as he saw it) in the 2009 election. He objects to American attempts to have members of his inner circle prosecuted for corruption, and he is deeply suspicious of American attempts to deal over his head with both the Pakistanis and the Taliban. Somewhat incongruously, President Karzai also apparently believes that the United States has unrevealed reasons to remain in Afghanistan indefinitely, beyond its concerns about Al Qaeda, and that Washington therefore remains committed to some kind of "victory" in Afghanistan.

The Kabul government's objectives in a peace process seem likely to include, roughly in this order,

- having President Karzai remain head of government until 2014 (and possibly thereafter) along with a guarantee of personal security for him, his family, and his inner circle, as well as immunity for some key allies
- the withdrawal of ISAF and American forces in an orderly, phased manner. They must provide training and weaponry to the Afghan army and police through 2014 and beyond.
- a peacekeeping force, provided by the international community for a limited period after an accord, that backfills the departing ISAF
- a resultant power-sharing arrangement that provides sufficient scope for non-Pashtun elements to forestall a renewed civil war along sectarian lines
- having Afghanistan remain a democratic state, and having its constitution survive largely intact. Some minority and gender rights could be introduced.
- continuing financial support provided to Afghanistan by the international community.

The first and second objectives are "must haves" for President Karzai and his inner circle, and the third is a "must have" for the former Northern Alliance figures. The pace of the ISAF drawdown may be negotiable from Kabul's standpoint, although it almost certainly must not conclude much earlier than the currently foreseen 2014 handover date. The terms of political restructuring, constitutional revision, the role of Islam, and methods for ensuring minority and gender rights are certainly negotiable. From Kabul's standpoint, the religious minority and gender protections aspect of the fourth objective could be compromised in the context of a top-level, three-way negotiation between the Karzai government, its Northern Alliance coalition members, and the Taliban. Civil society representatives will look to the international community to help ensure that these interests are protected.

President Karzai believes that only the United States can credibly deliver on the second objective (withdrawal) and that it will also be key to securing in the last objective (continued aid). The Europeans and the Japanese are also important actors in the long-run economic flow. President Karzai probably believes that the United States will be an obstacle to any extension of his term in office, although he may believe that a deal with the Taliban might include such a provision. He believes that the Pakistanis ultimately hold the key to achieving his first objective (security) through their leverage over the Quetta Shura and its affiliated insurgent networks.

President Karzai and his inner circle probably prefer first to arrive at a prior understanding with both the Taliban leadership and the Pakistani military, then to engage in a broader peace process. This broader process would likely include wider elements of the insurgency, probably beginning with the Quetta Shura, then incorporating the Hekmatyar network (with the Haqqani network being forced into the process by Islamabad), and finally involving the United States and the rest of the international community, who would be asked to endorse the resultant accord under some sort of UN umbrella. Kabul would depend on Washington and, to a lesser degree, Beijing to help ensure that Islamabad actually delivers on any concessions Pakistan might be inclined to grant Kabul, and Kabul will likely also depend on Islamabad to help make sure that the Taliban delivers on any actions it commits to undertake.

President Karzai wants a green light from the United States for negotiations with the Taliban and desires as few redlines as possible. He would also prefer to have a free hand to arrive at the terms of an understanding with Pakistan. A residual in-country American counterterrorist capability is notably absent from the Kabul government's list of objectives. Al Qaeda and other third-party terrorist groups are a tertiary concern of President Karzai and the Northern Alliance alike; it is violence perpetrated by Afghan terrorists (i.e., the Taliban) against Afghans that concerns them most.

If some American officials envisage the United States as necessary to brokering a peace agreement between Kabul and the Taliban, President Karzai probably sees his role as similarly central. Former U.S. Defense Department official and military expert Bing West has observed that "Karzai has behaved as if the war is between the United States and the Taliban, with the Afghan government a neutral party seeking a settlement."[13] Unless a greater degree of trust between the Karzai and Obama administrations can be fostered, their cooperation through a complex and lengthy peace process could be quite rocky. The lower the trust levels, the greater the levels of duplicity and evasion, and the more arm-twisting will be required to ink and then follow through on the terms of a peace accord.

President Karzai would also like the Chinese, the Europeans, the Japanese, the Turks, and all of the international financial institutions (such as the International Monetary Fund, the World Bank, and the Asian Development Bank) to keep aid funds flowing into Kabul's coffers for as long as possible. But sustaining the flow of foreign aid in the aftermath of a settlement is problematic. The international community is unlikely to continue current levels of assistance for long, and the even-greater spending associated with the NATO military presence will dry up as soon as Western forces begin departing (i.e., in 2011). It will be particularly difficult to generate public support in Europe and the United States for sustained economic assistance to Afghanistan if minority and gender rights are compromised or if the successor government takes on a more explicitly conservative Islamic coloration.

Given that Western troops are not likely to remain beyond 2014 in any significant numbers under any foreseeable circumstances, the prospect of more or less economic assistance is likely to be the international community's principal lever in influencing the outcome of negotiations on social and human rights issues. The Kabul government was never a fan of conditional aid. So, President Karzai (and his Taliban interlocutors) will likely put a premium on extracting aid commitments from non-NATO sources, including the international financial organizations, various deep-pocketed Persian Gulf entities, and, of course, the world's principal creditor nations, China and Japan.

---

[13] Bing West, *The Wrong War: Grit, Strategy, and the Way Out of Afghanistan*, New York: Random House, 2011, p. 251.

The Inner Ring

Pakistan

Pakistan's ultimate objectives in Afghanistan and the decisionmaking coherence of the Pakistani government are unclear, although we believe the latter to be low. There are two competing narratives about Pakistan's role in Afghanistan. Which one turns out to be true will have a profound effect on the negotiating process and on the ultimate outcome of any peace talks. If the government is divided, as seems most likely, the role Pakistan will ultimately play in any such process is even more unpredictable.

The first narrative, favored by many observers in Kabul, New Delhi, Washington, and even Islamabad, has Pakistan's security establishment viewing Afghanistan almost entirely through the prism of the Indian threat. In this narrative, Islamabad's principal objective in Afghanistan is to limit Indian influence, the risk of "encirclement," and Indian-supported subversion within Pakistan fomented from across the border in Afghanistan. In other words, the Pakistanis fear the Indians doing to them in the Baluch and Pashtun regions of Pakistan exactly what Pakistan has been doing to India in Kashmir for the past 60 years: undercutting sovereignty with proxy terrorists. To defend against this, Pakistan seeks a predominant role in Afghanistan for its Taliban proxies, even as it fights against the Pakistani Taliban at home. One Pakistani scholar describes this as the "security establishment's dual approach of practicing toughness towards home-grown terrorists and leniency towards home-based regional terrorists."[14]

According to this narrative, the Pakistanis want American forces to withdraw in an orderly fashion from Afghanistan; cease all unilateral intelligence gathering, special operations, and drone strikes in the border areas, and provide no-strings-attached financial and military aid to Pakistan. In short, they want a free hand on both sides of the Durand Line. One Pakistani military officer has explained his government's motivations as follows:

---

[14] Ishtiaq Ahmad, "The U.S. Af-Pak Strategy: Challenges and Opportunities for Pakistan," *Asian Affairs: An American Review*, Vol. 37, 2010, p. 192.

> It was the severity of the domestic terrorist threat that left Pakistan's civilian government and security establishment with no option but to undertake a resolute military offensive against domestic terrorist-insurgents like TTP and . . . [Tehrik-e-Nafaz-e-Shariat-e-Mohammadi]. That this development has brought about some compatibility between U.S. and Pakistani counterterrorism approaches during the time the . . . Afghanistan-Pakistan strategy has evolved or been implemented is, therefore, largely coincidental.[15]

Under this first narrative, Pakistan will, with whatever negative undertakings and lip service to a "neutral" Afghanistan are required, support a negotiated outcome that gives Washington and NATO a ticket out of the Afghan morass. After Washington and NATO are gone, Pakistan will resume its meddling and manipulation through its Taliban proxies, now members of a government of national reconciliation, with an eye toward countering any residual Iranian and Indian influence.

In this narrative, the Pakistanis have a reasonably unified policy view and believe that time is on their side. The national security establishment, meaning the military and its intelligence agencies, is in basic internal agreement with regard to Afghanistan and how to deal with Pakistan's own domestic TTP insurgency, and it is capable of designing and executing the necessary policies, despite the fact many other actors within Pakistan have very different views and objectives.

The competing, second narrative flips all of these points 180 degrees. In this view, professed by serious people in Islamabad and Washington and increasingly part of the Pakistani military's official line with foreign interlocutors, Pakistan now regards Afghanistan increasingly through the prism of the existential threat to the Pakistani state posed by the Pakistani Taliban rather than through the prism of an Indian threat. "We are the victims of extremist terrorism," goes this argument, pointing to the suicide bombings and brutal assassinations of civil, intelligence, and military figures carried out by Pakistan's own domestic insurgency. As a Pakistani journalist suggested to us,

---

[15] Ahmad, p. 203.

"Pakistan's military leadership has finally gotten the message that they are now in the gun sights of the jihadis, that the real risk to them is here in western Pakistan, not from the Indians in eastern Pakistan."

In this starkly different narrative, Islamabad does not control the Quetta Shura. It exercises some residual influence over the Taliban, but this influence is significantly attenuated. Because of this uneasy relationship with the Taliban, Pakistan wants a government in Kabul in which the Taliban participates but does not dominate. Instead, Islamabad wants Afghanistan stable enough that Pakistan can focus on its own domestic counterinsurgency. Pakistan wants to split the Afghan Taliban from the Pakistan Taliban, getting the former out of Pakistan by making it a junior partner in a Kabul government of national reconciliation while stamping out the latter at home. Islamabad therefore will do all in its power to nudge the Quetta Shura to the table, and it will honor its undertakings in any resultant accord. In this narrative, Pakistan wants the United States to withdraw its forces from Afghanistan (but in an orderly fashion) and to continue providing military and economic support to Pakistan so that the latter can wage its own domestic fight against extremism.

In this second narrative, Pakistani leaders do not believe that time is on their side. They recognize that Pakistan itself is now the prime locus of a militant extremist insurgency that poses an existential threat to the secular Pakistani state. Hence, Pakistan seeks urgently to close off the Afghanistan war in order to focus at home. A senior Pakistani legislator told us, "We have a window of opportunity to move against the TTP and other militant groups. For the first time, the people and politicians are aligned with the army in war against the TTP. We have had more casualties [due] to the TTP than to India."

This narrative also assumes that Pakistan is relatively coherent, at least with regard to national security objectives, and that the national security establishment's historical contacts with the Afghan Taliban can and will be severed in pursuit of this approach.

If this second narrative is the true portrait of Pakistan's position in Afghanistan, then Islamabad's objectives in an accord are, roughly in this order,

- a stable, reasonably neutral Kabul government with the Afghan Taliban as a junior partner
- Afghan and American support for counterterrorist and counter-insurgency operations against the Pakistani Taliban
- a phased American and NATO withdrawal from Afghanistan, but with continuing military and economic aid to Afghanistan thereafter
- limitations on, but not the complete elimination of, Indian influence and activities in Afghanistan, including effective checks on Indian capacity to support the anti-Pakistan insurgency in Baluchistan
- access to expanded trade with and investment in Afghanistan.

Of these five objectives, the first two are "must haves," the third and fourth are important but the terms flexible, and the last is a "nice to have."

On the other hand, if the first, darker narrative is the truer portrait of Pakistani intentions, then both the priority and the substance of these objectives changes to just three stark, simple "must haves":

- the entire cessation of Indian influence and activities in Afghanistan
- having Pakistan's Taliban allies play a major or dominant role in the Kabul government, allowing Pakistan to once again employ Afghan territory in training and organizing subversion against India
- the departure of the United States from Afghanistan and the cessation of drone strikes in Pakistan. However, the United States must continue to supply military and economic aid to Islamabad without conditions.

The second, more-positive narrative is more consistent with the Pakistani government's current pronouncements and also with Pakistani national interests, as seen from outside. Unfortunately, the first, less-constructive set of policies and objectives is more consistent with observed Pakistani behavior. As noted earlier, it is likely that both narratives have advocates within the Pakistan government and that the Pakistani strategy and decisionmaking unit with regard to Afghanistan is simply incoherent both vertically and horizontally. That is certainly the most charitable explanation for what otherwise seems to be conscious and concerted duplicity in Pakistani behavior.

As in the case of the Afghan Taliban, the ultimate Pakistani position on peace in Afghanistan is likely to emerge only once negotiations have begun. The prevailing narrative may switch in midstream or even oscillate over time. This means that Islamabad's objectives in a peace process may shift into and then out of alignment with those of Washington and Kabul. Any alignment may be temporary, and interests may be at cross-purposes at times. This will make Pakistan an extremely difficult party to deal with, both in negotiating and then in implementing any accord.

This obviously poses a major challenge for both Kabul and Washington, given that Islamabad, with a hard-to-read and possibly inconsistent set of policy goals that reflect deep and probably long-lasting differences inside the Pakistani establishment, is demanding a central role in any peace process, even in getting talks started. American negotiators will want to ensure that Pakistan's undertakings under any agreement are explicit and carefully spelled out in ways that make monitoring feasible and that provide for ongoing rewards for compliance and ongoing penalties for noncompliance. This will play out against the well-known backdrop of low mutual trust between Washington and Islamabad on almost all levels. Hard choices will have to be made in Washington with regard to the "strategic relationship" with Pakistan, whether things go well, badly, or nowhere in any peace process.

The Pakistanis almost certainly do not believe that the United States can credibly promise to limit Indian activities in Afghanistan, given the expanding security relationship between Washington and New Delhi. Only a new Afghan government can deliver on this limitation. If the first, darker narrative is correct, then this objective is at the top of Islamabad's list, and only a triangular agreement between President Karzai, the Afghan Taliban leadership, and Pakistan can ensure it. Indeed, the Afghan Taliban is the key party in actually delivering on most of the Pakistani objectives in Afghanistan, regardless of which narrative prevails.

There is much controversy and confusion about Pakistan's involvement with and control of its Afghan proxies. Pakistan has long-standing but complex historical relations with (and has periodically betrayed) the Taliban and its associated networks, including Hekmatyar and the Haqqani groups.

The Taliban depends on Pakistan's sanctuary for recruiting, rest and recuperation, and resupply. Many leaders of its various shura reside in Pakistan, and, in consequence, both they and their families are under continual threat of being jailed or expelled by Pakistani authorities. A retired Pakistani general told us, "The Taliban is not on good terms with the government of Pakistan. We have betrayed them, kept them under surveillance, put them in jail, kept their families hostage." Figures associated with the insurgency make the same points in decrying their dependence on Pakistan. Indeed, several Taliban military and political figures pointedly referred to the Pakistanis as "our jailors" in their conversations with us.

The Haqqani network is, of the groups in the insurgency, the one over which the Pakistani government appears to exercise the most direct influence. The government also has varying levels of influence among different factions of the Quetta Shura. In contrast, HiG has an on-again, off-again relationship with the ISI. HiG was Pakistan's favorite proxy in the 1990s, but the Pakistanis found Hekmatyar's military and political performance disappointing. Pakistan still retains some influence and some ability to rein Hekmatyar in, but it is not clear how much clout the Pakistanis have when it comes to HiG operations.

The Pakistanis have an incentive to exaggerate their control over the Afghan Taliban in order to strengthen their position in negotiations and to ensure that the final terms are as favorable to Pakistan as possible. As one Taliban district military commander told us, "The Pakistanis want to be asked by you to negotiate with us, and then they will insert their own demands and portray them as coming from us." On the other hand, the government of Pakistan pays a price with respect to American and European opinion every time it acknowledges links or influence over the Afghan insurgents because doing so reinforces the dark narrative of Pakistani complicity in the war and duplicity in Pakistan's relationship with NATO.

As a peace process gets started, Pakistani intelligence authorities are likely to use some active or former ISI operatives to approach Taliban leaders for their thoughts on the terms of a potential settlement. Indeed, certain members of the ISI have long been positioning themselves to take up this role. There are several senior or retired Pakistani officials who have long-standing ties and personal credibility with senior Taliban members. These officials, including Rustam Shah Mohmand, former chief secretary of the Northwest Frontier Province and High Commissioner to Afghanistan, and Lieutenant General (Ret.) Asad Durrani, former head of the ISI, could serve as effective go-betweens in a negotiation process.

The already ambivalent and conflicted relationship between Pakistan and the Afghan Taliban is likely to get even more tense, textured, and possibly violent as peace negotiations get under way. Islamabad holds many of the strong cards in this relationship, including sanctuary, some supplies, and the virtual hostage-holding of many Taliban leaders and their families. However, the Pakistanis also face a deep reservoir of Afghan resentment, even hatred. The Taliban could strike back at Pakistan, whether indirectly through the TTP or through its own networks among the extensive Pashtun Diaspora that stretches from Peshawar to Karachi—something it has, to date, refrained from doing.

On balance, Pakistan would probably prefer to deal with Mullah Omar directly—and with other members of the Quetta Shura who reside in Pakistan—rather than with former Taliban diplomats, such as Mullah Abdul Salam Zaeef (between whom and Pakistan there is bad blood) and Mullah Wakil Muttawakil, both of whom currently reside in Kabul. In fact, it has been widely alleged that the arrest of Mullah Beradar Akhond, one of Mullah Omar's top lieutenants, was a signal to both the Taliban and the Karzai government that Pakistan discourages any direct negotiations between Kabul and insurgency leadership that are not brokered by Islamabad. So, one of the most important tasks in launching a peace process will be to win some space in Pakistan for the

Taliban to engage in serious negotiations without being jailed by the ISI.

Pakistan has extensive, although not particularly encouraging, experience in sending representatives into the FATA to negotiate ceasefires and peace accords with its own militant groups. Pakistan used a network of traditional jirgas, ulema, and academics to support these negotiations and help secure the subsequent approval of resultant agreements.

Pakistan would prefer that India have no standing in peace negotiations, and it would prefer that negotiations take place in such a venue as Kabul, Riyadh, or perhaps Istanbul. In addition, Pakistan is likely to seek support and guarantees from China and from some key members of the Organization of the Islamic Conference for the monitoring and implementation of any agreement.

The military establishment in Pakistan regards itself as the key decisionmaker and final arbitrator on security issues, including the terms of a possible peace accord. Thus, there will be no successful negotiation without the participation of the Pakistani military, including its intelligence arm, the ISI. Key current and former officers of the ISI are Pakistan's best channels to the Taliban, particularly those who have long-standing personal relationships with the insurgent leadership. Other, newer ISI officers do not have the same influence or access. There is a multiplicity of views within the Pakistan military regarding Afghanistan strategy, and there will be an ongoing debate among the Corps Commanders of the Pakistani Armed Forces over the pace and outcome of a peace process.

Civilian politicians have no real purchase over issues that are central to Pakistan's national security, at least not yet. However, the death of Bin Laden and the high-profile TTP attacks on Pakistani military targets, such as the Mehran naval base, have given Pakistan's civilian leaders some leverage over the military, and civilian leaders have taken an increasingly prominent role in meetings between Pakistani and Afghan leaders. Civilian politicians will expect to be consulted on the general terms of any accord as it is broached and negotiated. Civilian Pakistani political leaders who accompanied senior military leaders on a visit to Kabul in spring 2011 seem to have taken center stage in those talks, suggesting that the two groups have arrived at some sort of consensus with regard to Afghanistan strategy, at least for the moment. If it were to contain any formal undertakings for Pakistan, a peace agreement would need to be approved by majority vote in Pakistan's National Assembly and Senate, or, conceivably, by an All Party Conference.

Public opinion in Pakistan remains overwhelmingly against the presence of American and other foreign forces in Afghanistan; most Pakistanis see this presence as a destabilizing influence in their own country. Public opinion favors a negotiated settlement with the Afghan Taliban but is very hostile toward the Pakistani Taliban. Indeed, bloody attacks by the Pakistani militants—especially suicide bombings with great loss of civilian life—have dramatically reduced public support for homegrown jihadi groups. Video images and other reporting on the imposition of fundamentalist rule by local militants, including canings and other atrocities, have also turned public sentiment against these groups.

Potential spoilers to a peace accord include Al Qaeda and other extremist groups, including foreign militant groups from Uzbekistan and elsewhere in Central Asia, who will react violently to any threat to their safe heavens in southern and eastern Afghanistan and in the bordering FATA. Splinter groups within splinter groups in the border areas have cross-cutting rivalries, blood-feuds, and tribal cleavages, constituting a witches' brew of Islamic extremism, Pashtun nationalism, and banditry. Any of these groups under the nominal banner of the Pakistani Taliban could unleash further attacks in Pakistan's major cities at any time. In turn, the Pakistanis will unleash their own allies within the tribes and other proxies against the Pakistani Taliban. It will be very hard to keep track of the players and the subgames influencing Pakistani behavior.

Pakistan does not seem to have a timeline or calendar for an accord. Much turns on whether the Pakistanis believe time to be on their side, and the answer to that question depends on which narrative dominates Pakistani policy at any particular moment. Another important timing factor involves Pakistani counterinsurgency operations in the FATA. If and when the Pakistani army moves into North

Waziristan, an offensive long promised and oft delayed on the grounds
that it must be carefully prepared, one can expect violent reprisals by
the Pakistani militants in the frontier regions and in Pakistan's capital
and large cities. Such a move by Pakistani forces into the frontier areas
would, nevertheless, put new pressure on the Afghan Taliban.

The United States

The United States has multiple goals in Afghanistan, roughly in this
order:

- preventing Afghanistan from becoming a sanctuary for and an
  ally of Al Qaeda, as it was under the Taliban
- creating a reasonably stable, autonomous, and friendly state in
  Afghanistan
- preventing Afghan violence from further destabilizing Pakistan
- preserving democratic and human rights for Afghans
- preserving the credibility of the NATO alliance
- reducing the illicit drug trade.

The lines of disagreement within the American foreign policy–making
process regarding the priority of these objectives and the resources
required to achieve them are well documented in the media.

The first objective (expelling Al Qaeda) was the original reason
for the American intervention in Afghanistan and is the main reason
President Obama has cited for sustaining and indeed increasing the
American military commitment. This objective is a "must have." The
second objective is derivative of the first. The third (Pakistani stability) emerged after the intervention had taken place and is now seen by
many as the most critical American interest in the region. The fourth
objective (democratization) is a core American value, but one often
compromised when too difficult or too expensive to secure. The last
two objectives are essentially "nice to haves." Damage to NATO has
already been incurred, and the terms of a peace accord may make little
difference on that score. The United States is a secondary or even tertiary market for Afghan's heroin production, and, in any case, any

reduction in supply from Afghanistan will likely be offset by some other producer.

Washington will have to engage in any peace process against the noisy backdrop of bureaucratic warfare, partisan sniping, congressional second-guessing, apparently unpluggable leaking, and an intrusive and critical media. Afghanistan and its immediate neighbors have no monopoly on incoherence.

Most Americans understand that the international community must help build a minimally capable Afghan state and continue to provide military and economic assistance to Kabul over time in order to sustain the first objective. But, in an era of economic retrenchment and intervention fatigue, Americans are likely to accept greater risk of failure in Afghanistan as the price for a reduced commitment of American resources. The laudable goal of creating a democratic Afghan state with economic development, the rule of law, and religious, gender, and minority rights is likely to be scaled back as the price for so doing becomes more burdensome and the memory of 9/11 recedes. Within the executive branch, Vice President Joe Biden has repeatedly expressed his preference for a strategy in Afghanistan that focuses more exclusively on the counterterrorism goal in both Afghanistan and Pakistan rather than an open-ended commitment to counterinsurgency and state-building in Afghanistan.

The President of the United States will ultimately decide on what is vital and what is merely desirable in terms of an accord. The President will seek agreement among the National Security Council principals (primarily the Secretaries of State and Defense) and solicit input from the intelligence agencies and the uniformed military while also keeping an eye on domestic American opinion and the electoral calendar. Coordinating the political, military, and intelligence arms of American efforts in Afghanistan will take strong direction and leadership from the White House. It will also take a good deal of public relations discipline for the American government and its negotiators to stay "on message" about the objectives and terms of an accord. Leaks and criticism, particularly when inspired by those whose views may be overruled in the Situation Room, could seriously undermine a negotiation and even sink an agreement.

There is considerable antipathy toward the Afghan war among many members of the Democratic caucus, and there is deep skepticism of President Obama's national security strategy among many members of the Republican Party. Congress exerts influence through hearings and appropriations bills and so would have to be kept in the loop, to some degree, regarding any talks. The Senate would need to ratify any resultant treaty to which the United States was a party, and both Houses would need to deliver on any financial commitments.

When negotiations begin, the Kabul government, Pakistan, and even NATO—not to mention the United States' nominal adversaries, the Taliban and the Iranians—are likely to have a low level of trust in American intentions. There is also a long line of states waiting to pick Washington's pocket as the price for helping it get out of Afghanistan. At the head of the line are the Karzai government and the Pakistanis, both of which are skilled in extracting money and resources from Washington and almost certainly see peace negotiations as an opportunity to extract even greater sums from the United States as the "price" of an accord that meets even minimal American objectives. The Iranians, the Russians, and the Chinese may seek concessions from the United States to secure their assistance in a peace process, or even just to abstain from blocking it. The Saudis, the Turks, and some Europeans may be willing to contribute political capital to this exercise, but probably not on a large enough scale to make a major difference. At the end of the day, Pakistan exercises an effective veto on whether any accord will indeed fulfill the top American goal in Afghanistan. Tehran could also make it very hard, if it chose, but only at some expense in terms of its own interests, which actually coincide with Washington's on most points.

As we have repeatedly observed, the low coherence of both the Taliban and the Karzai government is a major challenge for the United States in terms of forging a credible negotiating process. The weak Karzai government has posed a basic problem for the United States and its NATO allies in the conduct of the war for almost a decade, and that problem has worsened with the Coalition's explicit adoption of a counterinsurgency strategy in recent years. To be successful, counterinsurgency requires a reasonably legitimate and at least minimally capable indigenous state that can be defended against insurgency. The United States and its allies have sought to improve the performance of the Kabul regime but with only mixed results to date.

As noted earlier, the structural incoherence and possible duplicity of Pakistan pose a major challenge. At some point, the divergence between American and Pakistani objectives in Afghanistan may come to a head. Although another "You're with us or against us," 9/11-like moment may not occur again, at some point it will become evident which of the two narratives dominates Pakistani policy, and, if the wrong answer emerges, the American-Pakistani relationship may take a very sharp nosedive.

The United States labors under a tight time constraint of its own making. Although President Obama has effectively shifted the focus of withdrawal from 2011 to 2014, this ticking clock puts a real burden on American negotiators in any peace process. The temporal question for American policymakers is thus not "Is time on our side?" but rather "How much can we achieve before we run out of time?"

It is striking how many of the other parties to a peace accord have a longer timeline than that of the United States. Almost all of the regional actors can play the long game in Afghanistan. In contrast, American influence in Afghanistan is on a gradually declining trajectory. The ability to modulate violence in order to bring the Taliban to the negotiating table (and to keep it there) is a wasting asset. Gradually declining American leverage means that the longer it takes to negotiate any peace agreement, the less influence the United States is likely to have over its contents. It would be hard today for the United States to offer to accelerate its planned withdrawal in exchange for other considerations (e.g., a Taliban break with Al Qaeda), and it will soon be practically impossible. The slope of the declining trajectory may be gradual for a while, and it may even be altered with mini-surges if those become necessary to maintaining negotiating leverage at some points in the process, but it probably cannot be credibly reversed indefinitely.

If the leaders of the insurgency still believe in the oft-quoted quip that "ISAF has all the watches but we have the time," then only considerable improvement in the performance of the Afghan security forces, and the Kabul government more broadly, is likely to change their mind.

Some Taliban figures may prove willing to negotiate, and others may prefer to wait out ISAF. To the degree that intelligence sources can distinguish between these different groups, both vertically and horizontally, then special operations forces raids and drones might be employed in ways that encourage the would-be peacemakers and isolate or eliminate the bitter-enders. This will be harder to do if the principal cleavage within the insurgency is vertical, with the Quetta Shura inclined to negotiate while local district commanders prefer to fight on. On the other hand, if there are local commanders on the ground who are willing to settle but it is the Quetta Shura that is resisting, it will still be difficult to shape a definitive outcome, but there will be a better chance of at least reducing the overall threat posed by the insurgency by encouraging defections.

One of the basic precepts of competent negotiation is to always keep the best alternative to no agreement clearly in mind and to reject any accord that does not improve on it. In Afghanistan, the best alternative to a peace agreement would be a regime in Kabul that is able to sustain itself indefinitely against the Taliban with much lower levels of American support. To the extent that the United States and its allies succeed in efforts to so improve the capacity of the Afghan army, police, and government, they both enhance their negotiating position and create an acceptable alternative to failure to achieve an agreement.

The First Ring

India

India's strategy toward Pakistan is reasonably coherent both vertically and horizontally, subject to the checks and balances characteristic of any fractious, internally focused liberal democracy. It is hard to keep a diplomatic secret in most liberal democracies, and particularly with a free media, such as India's.

The Prime Minister and his National Security Advisor, and perhaps also the Foreign Minister, will be the key decisionmakers in any Afghan peace process. The Prime Minister might try keep such negotiations very close, possibly even cutting out the Foreign Ministry bureaucracy and working through the National Security Advisor for a period of time. The intelligence apparatus, principally the Research and Analysis Wing of the Indian Cabinet Secretariat, would provide key inputs to the process, given the salience of Pakistan and the terrorism problem in any Afghan negotiations. Unlike the military establishment in Pakistan, Indian armed forces are not sufficiently involved in Afghan policy to have a major say in any Afghan political settlement.

Once formal negotiations begin, Indian representation would probably be accomplished through the Foreign Ministry's regular channels, under the direction of the Foreign Minister and his most senior career staff. India has quite a number of skilled diplomats with ample experience and exposure to Afghanistan. India would prefer that negotiations take place in a traditional neutral European capital, such as Geneva, or possibly even in Turkey, and would be less happy with a venue that has strong Islamic overtones, such as Riyadh or Doha.

The governing party and Parliament would need to approve any accord that formally binds India. The opposition will almost certainly critique India's participation in a peace process; minority members of the governing coalition might also defect if they became too unhappy with the direction taken by negotiations. If the Hindu nationalist Bharatiya Janata Party is still in opposition, it will likely focus on the risk that any agreement might strengthen Pakistan and empower Islamic terrorist groups. On the other hand, in India's tumultuous, coalition-based political system, some Muslim communities comprise local but strategic vote banks that are necessary for certain coalitions to survive. Indian political figures—particularly in the Congress Party—have been and will remain loath to inflame the sentiments of these important constituencies. Public opinion in India will nevertheless be generally averse to the inclusion of the Taliban or any other Islamic radical groups in a new Afghan governing structure.

Indian officials are very skeptical about the utility of Afghan peace talks but will want to be present if they occur. The Indians would prefer to see such negotiations organized within a UN context. India does not have a specific timetable for an Afghan "solution." Top Indian political figures are upset by the timeline for NATO withdrawal from Afghanistan and by what they consider to be a failure of American resolve, fearing a "retreat" that "will leave India holding the bag," as one senior diplomat told us.

India's foreign policy priorities—or, at least, India's ability to marshal the energy and attention needed to engage seriously in such a foreign policy issue as Afghanistan—rise and fall with cabinets in the uncertain parliamentary election cycles. India's approach will also be importantly influenced by the state of bilateral talks (or tensions) between New Delhi and Islamabad.

India's goals in an Afghan peace process include, more or less in this order,

- a friendly or at least neutral Afghan government that is not dominated by the Taliban or other Pakistani proxies
- elimination of Al Qaeda and other Islamist terrorist group sanctuaries in Afghanistan, although it is Pakistani terrorist groups who target India that are of primary concern to New Delhi
- preservation of an Indian presence in Afghanistan, including a political and military intelligence capability, partly as a mechanism for ensuring that the first two objectives are enforced over time but also to maintain India's broader influence in the Central Asia region
- expansion of Indian trade with and investment in Afghanistan, including access to transit routes through both Pakistan and Iran
- preservation of basic human rights for Afghans
- maintaining and strengthening India's growing strategic partnership with the United States.

The first two goals are vital for India, the third is important principally as a means to ensure the first two, and the last three goals are "nice to haves." Afghanistan is small potatoes for an emerging economic giant like India, and India is already tolerating severe human rights oppression in other near neighbors, such as Burma, Iran, and Sri Lanka.

Much to the discomfort of Indian diplomats, Pakistan plays the key role in delivering on four of these six objectives. India will press for some acknowledgment of its security interests in any accord and will insist that the result not facilitate Pakistan's ability to support terrorist attacks on India in Kashmir and beyond. This could well be the subject of a parallel side agreement between New Delhi and Islamabad, whether public or private.

On this score, some observers suggest that the United States should attempt to promote an Indian-Pakistani rapprochement on Kashmir as part of an Afghan settlement strategy. We believe this objective to be highly desirable but an unrealistically ambitious undertaking that is analogous to solving the Israeli-Palestinian problem. At the end of the day, statesmen in Islamabad and New Delhi will have to arrive at some conclusion or at least a modus vivendi on their own terms; encouragement from Washington should continue but is unlikely to have more than a marginal effect on the behavior of either party. Potential spoilers to India's involvement in a peace process include the domestic Indian opposition party at the time and, possibly, internal or external terrorist groups, although one hopes that Pakistan will exercise some degree of control over its proxy terrorist entities (such as Lashkar-e-Taiba) during a negotiation. As noted earlier, spoilers inside Pakistan who object to Islamabad's engagement in a peace accord are entirely capable of striking against New Delhi rather than against Islamabad, knowing that inflaming the Indian-Pakistani tensions is an effective way to reduce the odds of a successful peace accord. Keeping Afghanistan negotiations on track while enduring bloody terrorist attacks at home will require remarkable forbearance and political courage on the part of Indian statesmen.

India has traditionally allied itself with the former Northern Alliance against the Taliban and has close ties with many of its senior members, both in the Kabul government and in the opposition. At the end of the day, if India's leaders believe that negotiations imperil either of India's top two objectives, they could derail the process by encouraging their own proxy groups in Afghanistan to oppose the emerging agreement, defect from the Kabul government, or even take up arms against it. The United States will be obliged to send repeated and clear messages of reassurance to the Indians in order to forestall this outcome.

Iran

Iran may have high horizontal coherence with regard to its objectives in Afghanistan, but it is very hard to tell from the outside. As with many other matters of foreign policy, Iran's position with regard to a peace process is likely to be obscured by political infighting in Tehran among lay political leaders, clerics, members of the Islamic Revolutionary Guard Corps (IRGC), conservatives, and those few reformers not in prison. There is probably less vertical coherence in Iran's strategy toward Afghanistan, given all the cross-cutting interests of various Iranian groups in Afghan trade and investment, drug trafficking, refugee and labor migration, criminal groups, and multiple (and sometimes conflicting) lines of support to Iran's many proxies inside the country.

Supreme Leader Ali Khamenei will have the final say on Iran's negotiating strategy. The executive branch of the Iranian government, led by President Mahmud Ahmadinejad, will be involved in the negotiation through the Foreign Ministry and other senior individuals reporting to the President's office. Elements of the Quds Force of the IRGC will probably also play key roles. Veto power rests exclusively with Supreme Leader Khamenei, but formal approval must be officially obtained from the Iranian parliament for any formal undertakings.

History suggests that, until formal negotiations begin (at which point, the Iranian delegation would sort itself out), parallel lines of competing authority may emerge as the Iranian government becomes involved in peace discussions. Iran would involve both civilian and military personnel in such negotiations, with Minister of Foreign Affairs Ali Akbar Salehi and Iran's ambassador in Afghanistan, Feda Hussein Maliki, likely to play major roles, and with ample representation from the IRGC in any delegation.

There are several possible spoilers within the Iranian system, given the opaque decisionmaking process, multiple parallel actors, and high level of internal contention for authority. These spoilers may include elements within the Quds Force, should they disagree with the terms of an emerging accord. If prominent Hazara, Tajik, or Uzbek figures in Afghanistan perceive their interests to be threatened in a prospective agreement, they will likely turn to Iran for support. Conversely, there is some risk that indigenous Iranian insurgent groups will try to disrupt any peace process that would serve to strengthen the Iranian regime.

Iran has traditionally allied itself with and supported most Northern Alliance groups and has thus both cooperated and competed with India for the allegiance of those groups. Iran also has a special relationship with the Hazara, the Heratis, and other smaller Shia groups inside Afghanistan. Although Iran has supplied limited support and weapons to some Taliban groups in the past, it is not clear how strong this influence remains. Iran has played both sides of the Afghan conflict, maintained deep ties with those in the Kabul leadership, and supplied cash to President Karzai and others in his government for years. Iran is also a major aid donor to Afghanistan, with many of its projects devoted to development in western Afghanistan, which borders Iran. As a result, Herat and the surrounding area are some of the most prosperous and peaceful lands in the country. On balance, Tehran probably has relatively limited leverage with the Taliban leadership in any negotiations, but it has extensive experience in building up and manipulating proxies as a tool of policy, as evidenced by its relationship with Hamas in Gaza and with Hezbollah in Lebanon.

Iran will likely adopt a passive role in the run-up to any accord negotiations, continue to fulminate against UN and American involvement in Afghanistan, and use indirect pressure through its proxies. If the negotiating forum gives neighboring states some standing, Iran is likely to show up. Its behavior would be heavily conditioned by the state of its relations with the United States. Thus, Iran could prove quite unhelpful for reasons extraneous to Afghanistan, despite the fact that Iranian and American interests with regard to that country are rather closely aligned.

Given the recently warm relations between Tehran and Ankara, Turkey might be Iran's preferred venue for peace talks. Riyadh or one of the Persian Gulf capitals would be problematic because of high and rising tensions between several of the Sunni Gulf monarchies and Iran.

Iran does not seem to have any timeline or calendar pressures for an Afghan settlement. If anything, the Iranians appear fairly satisfied with a stalemate status quo in Afghanistan, one that ties down American armed forces, holds them hostage to possible Iranian indirect violence through IRGC proxies in Afghanistan, and plays into the narrative of the United States as "waging war on Islam." However, the Iranians appear to fear any permanent, postaccord American military presence in Afghanistan and will presumably use all the levers at their disposal to oppose any terms that would permit this. The rhythm of Iranian support for or obstruction of a peace process is more likely to depend on timelines external to Afghanistan, such as progress in Iran's nuclear program, competition between Iran and the Gulf states, and Iran's long-standing tensions with the United States.

Iran's objectives in Afghanistan include, roughly in this order,

- the eventual withdrawal of American and ISAF military and intelligence forces from Afghanistan
- a stable Afghanistan with a regime in Kabul that is friendly to Iran and not dominated by Pakistan or Pakistan's Taliban proxies
- protection of the interests of traditional Iranian allies inside Afghanistan, such as Farsiwan Heratis, Shia Hazara, and Tajiks, from Taliban revenge
- trade with and investment in Afghanistan, including transit trade through Chabar and possible future gas pipelines
- return to Afghanistan of the remaining 2 million–3 million Afghan refugees currently in Iran
- reduction in narcotics flows into and through Iran
- Kabul's cooperation in fighting the Jundallah (the Peoples Islamic Movement of Iran) insurgency.

The first two objectives are strategic and "must haves." The last five are important but negotiable "nice to haves," stemming as they do from geography and from the ebb and flow of trade, people, narcotics, and even terrorists across the Afghan-Iranian mutual border; these are matters that literally come with the territory. Although a peace accord may make some gestures in these directions or even contain some provisions relating to all seven of these Iranian objectives, the underlying problems will be around for a long time, and Tehran will not look to an Afghan peace process to solve them.

Iran would be cautious about accepting any undertakings resulting from a negotiated settlement process, but it also would not want to be left on the sidelines. It would favor a minimal international role in Afghanistan postsettlement, although it would probably find non-Western peacekeeping forces preferable to a continued American and NATO military presence.

Russia

Russia's strategy toward Afghanistan and a prospective peace accord is reasonably coherent, painfully informed by recent history, and largely negative in terms of its objectives. According to analysts Dmitri Trenin and Alexey Malashenko,

> Moscow sees its policies towards Afghanistan not as something shaped by the public good, such as helping to end the fighting or to restore peace and stability in the region. Rather, they are a means of bolstering Russia's geopolitical position and gaining material advantage. Afghanistan is also a bargaining chip in Russia's wider relations with the United States. . . . In the Russian political mind, rational calculations of interests and analyses of threats are superimposed, of course, on the Soviet Union's traumatic experience in Afghanistan—the "Afghan syndrome"—and on the post-Soviet Russian experience in Chechnya, Dagestan, Ingushetia, and Tajikistan.[16]

This formulation of Russian interests and the historical trauma that informs them is shared by all senior Russian policymakers, including Prime Minister Vladimir Putin. Russian military and intelligence veterans vividly remember Afghanistan as a brutal bloodletting of the Soviet Union masterminded by the United States. In discussions, a former Russian intelligence officer repeatedly referred to the Taliban as "your mujahidin."

Russian goals in Afghanistan include, roughly in this order,

---

[16] Dmitri Trenin and Alexey Malashenko, *Afghanistan: A View from Moscow*, Washington, D.C.: Carnegie Endowment, 2010.

- countering the ability of Islamic extremist groups to support Chechens or to engage in terrorist acts inside Russia or against Russian interests abroad
- eliminating the American and NATO military presence in Central Asia, including access to airbases in Kyrgyzstan and elsewhere in the region
- reducing the flow of heroin from Afghanistan to Russia
- blocking development of gas and oil pipelines from Central Asia south through Afghanistan.

There is a slight conflict between the first two goals: The Russians would like the United States gone from Afghanistan, but Moscow probably realizes that some residual American intelligence or special operations presence may be necessary to ensure the implementation of any counterterrorist undertakings resulting from a peace accord. In this sense, the Russian position toward a peace process is caught in a dilemma of sorts. As a Russian former Soviet Army officer said, "We want you to suffer and retreat in Afghanistan the way you forced us to, yet we don't want you to lose so badly that you empower Al Qaeda and Islamic extremists."

This suggests that Russia could be either marginally helpful or marginally obstructive in any peace negotiations. The Russians have been willing to provide temporary transit accommodations to ISAF in order to blunt Pakistani threats to ISAF's logistical supply lines, and they have temporarily suspended their efforts to limit American access to Central Asian basing and transit. But, at the end of the day, one of the primary benefits to Moscow of a successful peace process is the exit of American military forces and the reduction of Washington's political influence throughout Central Asia.

The Second Ring

Turkey

Turkey has multiple interests that would be served by a successful peace process, and it could well play a central role in helping to bring about such an accord. Turkey's government is also reasonably coherent on these issues. Ankara's relations with the parties to the conflict, and its understanding of the context, are extensive.

Turkey is the only country that has maintained reasonably good relations with all of the potential parties to a peace process. Ankara's relations with the Kabul government and with various leaders of the former Northern Alliance are close. Yet, Turkey also had reasonably good relations with the Taliban when it was in power. Even now, Ankara can probably activate personal ties with some Taliban leaders, which is pretty remarkable for a NATO member that has, from the beginning, contributed troops to ISAF.

Prime Minister Recep Tayyip Erdoğan, President Abdullah Gül, and their inner circle will be the central Turkish players in negotiations on any peace process for Afghanistan. A prominent role for Turkey in bringing about an accord would have a positive political impact for Prime Minister Erdoğan and for his Justice and Development Party. There is unlikely to be significant disagreement over Turkey's goals in Afghanistan in the political opposition or among the military.

Ankara's proxies in the Afghan conflict include the Uzbeks, notably General Dostum, and the Junbesh movement. It also has close ties with the Turkmens and a few other groups allied with the former Northern Alliance. Ankara exerts a modest degree of control over these proxies that is based on suasion, trust, intercessions with the Karzai government, and some financial support. Turkish officials claim to have terminated their relationship with General Dostum, but refuge in Turkey could again become an attractive possibility to the general if he no longer feels welcome in Afghanistan.

Turkey's goals in Afghanistan include, roughly in this order,

- fighting terrorism. Turkey is a frontline state that has experienced numerous terrorist attacks and casualties, including those due to or related to Al Qaeda
- expanding commerce. Turkish firms are major participants in construction and development contracts in Afghanistan, and Turkey is a large foreign investor in the region.

- promoting Turkish political influence and prestige throughout Central Asia
- protecting the interests of Turkic ethnic groups, such as the Uzbeks and Turkmens
- strengthening Turkey's role in NATO. A leadership role for Ankara in stabilizing Afghanistan would contrast with the slack created by the lack of leadership exhibited by several other NATO members.

Turkey will be well served by *any* reasonable accord. There are few obvious sticking points; Ankara's diplomats will not need to carefully craft the terms of the accord in order for it to be acceptable at home. The greater the Turkish role in facilitating agreement, the greater the domestic political payout for Prime Minister Erdoğan. This makes Turkey an attractive host or mediator in a peace process for Afghanistan.

Saudi Arabia

Saudi Arabia's influence and interest in Afghanistan stems from Riyadh's long association with the mujahidin in the anti-Soviet conflict and its relatively warm relationship with the IEA when the Taliban controlled most of Afghanistan. There was a notorious falling out between Saudi Arabia and the IEA when Mullah Omar allegedly promised to hand over Bin Laden and then reneged, but the Taliban still relies heavily on private donations from wealthy Persian Gulf individuals to conduct the war, and, as Guardian of the Two Holy Mosques, the House of Saud has influence with the Taliban.

The King and the senior Saudi Princes will be the ultimate decisionmakers regarding any peace process, and there is likely to be considerable coherence in Saudi Arabia's goals for Afghanistan, which are countering both Al Qaeda and Iran and contributing to the stability of Pakistan, an important Saudi ally.

Al Qaeda is a sworn enemy of the Saudi state and of the Al Saud family (which amount to virtually the same thing). Émigré Saudi terrorists cycling through Afghanistan and Pakistan pose a continuing threat to Saudi Arabia and to its neighbors in the Gulf states and

Yemen. The Saudis will have no objection to the extension of sharia law or to the imposition of conservative religious practices as the price for a peace settlement. On the contrary, Saudi public opinion (at least male Saudi public opinion) likely favors a settlement in Afghanistan that includes extensive Islamicization, more-conservative social policies, steps back from popular democracy, (possibly) full sharia law, and "rehabilitation" of the Taliban as part of a power-sharing arrangement. Riyadh is also likely to favor the eventual withdrawal of Western forces. The American military presence in Afghanistan continues to feed the perception of a war against Islam, a narrative that animates anti-Americanism and strains the U.S.-Saudi security relationship.

Riyadh has no particular time pressure with regard to Afghanistan, and its relationship with Washington has suffered recently as a result of the "Arab Spring." The regime nevertheless has little to risk and possibly modest gains to achieve by hosting peace negotiations. It would likely be willing to exercise its moral suasion—and perhaps a limited amount of checkbook diplomacy—to nudge Kabul and the Taliban toward signing an agreement.

China

There are several striking similarities between Chinese and Russian goals in Afghanistan. China is a formidably coherent decisionmaking unit whose goals for any accord are generally negative. Primarily, it wants to get the United States out of Central Asia. In the interim, both China and Russia, two great powers close to Afghanistan, have not been entirely displeased to see the United States and its NATO allies being ground down in a extended military stalemate in Central Asia.

On the other hand, China, unlike Russia, has not traditionally been a major player of the Afghan "Great Game." It has no strong ties with any of the Afghan factions, it is not embittered by a previous defeat, and its primary objectives are to limit the spread of Muslim militancy throughout Central Asia and to advance its commercial interests, including access to Afghanistan's natural resources. In this sense, Chinese diplomats are probably viewing Afghanistan through the geopolitical lens of China's own South Asian "Great Game," since Beijing's fundamental position in Afghanistan is going to be shaped more by

China's desire to counterbalance India and support Pakistan than by any direct Chinese stakes in Afghanistan. The Chinese are unlikely to exert themselves in support of a peace process, but they are unlikely to obstruct it, as long as Pakistan is adequately included.

The Standing Committee of the Politburo will base Chinese policy regarding Afghanistan on the recommendations of the Foreign Ministry and on input from both the People's Liberation Army and the Ministry of State Security. Several members of the Standing Committee are deeply experienced in Central Asia. For example, Zhou Yongkang was the founding chief of the PetroChina Tarim Oilfield Company from 1988 to 1990, when he concurrently served as deputy general manager of PetroChina. Zhou later served in the key post of Minister of Public Security. Wang Lequan, the former Party Chief of Xinjiang, worked in Afghanistan from 1991 to 2000, and another Politburo member, Wang Gang, served as a *mishu* [personal assistant] in the general office of the Xinjiang Party Committee from 1977 to 1981.

Vice Foreign Minister Dai Bingguo will likely take a close interest in both accord negotiations and their outcome. He can draw on a cadre of skilled professional diplomats who have served in the Central Asia 'Stans, Afghanistan, or Pakistan. Like current Chinese Ambassador to Afghanistan Zheng Qingdian, former ambassadors, especially Yang Houlan (serving from 2007 to 2009; now in charge of North Korea issues in the Foreign Ministry) and Liu Jian (serving from 2005 to 2007), are frequently consulted. Another diplomat who is likely to be consulted is Zhang Deguang, who served in multiple posts in Central Asia and was appointed head of the Shanghai Cooperation Organisation in 2004.

China's objectives in Afghanistan include, roughly in this order,

- eliminating the Western military presence in Afghanistan and Central Asia
- curbing the ability of Islamic extremist groups (such as the East Turkistan Islamic Movement) to support Uyghurs or to engage in terrorist acts in China or against Chinese interests
- supporting Pakistan (China's oldest and most trusted ally) and insulate it from instability in Afghanistan

- reducing both Russian and Indian influence in Central Asia
- ensuring access to raw materials (such as natural gas and metals) from Afghanistan. China Metallurgical Corporation's Mes Anyak copper project is the first of what will probably be many natural resource investment projects that China will undertake in Afghanistan if the security situation is sufficiently resolved by a peace accord.
- strengthening the role of the Shanghai Cooperation Organisation in the region.

The Chinese have no specific timelines with regard to an Afghan settlement. Their objectives are all long term, and, presumably, so is their perspective on a peace process. Chinese diplomacy in any case tends to be cautious and largely reactive. The next major inflection point in China's policymaking calendar is the transition from fourth-generation leadership (Hu Jintao, Wen Jiabao, Zeng Qinghong, et al.) to fifth-generation leadership (Xi Jinping, Li Keqiang, Bo Xilai, et al.), currently scheduled to take place at the 18th Communist Party Congress in fall 2012. There, the composition of the Politburo and its Standing Committee will be reshuffled, resulting (with some time lag) in the replacement of a large number of senior bureaucrats, provincial leaders, top People's Liberation Army generals, and foreign policy advisers. However, the institutional coherence of the Chinese foreign policymaking apparat will almost certainly ensure long-term consistency in Beijing's Afghan policies.

Europe

European governments sustain some limited horizontal coherence in their approach to Afghanistan through NATO and European Union machinery, but they otherwise speak with many voices, which could well become a confusing babble in the context of a peace process.

The senior NATO civilian representative in Kabul serves as a sort of diplomatic consigliere for the ISAF commander, but his capacity to coordinate the diplomatic activity of member governments is limited because there is a continual jostling for influence among all the local ambassadors, the many other international organizations with prominent European participation (most notably, NATO, the European Union, and the UN agencies), and the steady stream of senior officials from Brussels and other European capitals. As a result of these multiple contact points, the Europeans are likely to maintain a high level of awareness of peace discussions and are probably eager to play a role in facilitating an accord; their problem is maintaining one voice once negotiations become serious.

Despite this institutional incoherence, the Europeans are largely united with respect to their basic objectives in Afghanistan. Europeans do not believe that time is on their side, militarily speaking. Each country is committed to varying but generally short-term deadlines for the withdrawal of their combat forces, although a few may be ready to maintain a security assistance and training role beyond 2014. Public opinion is solidly behind this departure. Even a large terrorist strike in Europe is highly unlikely to change public opinion, since forensic and other evidence is more likely to tie such an attack to Pakistani, Middle Eastern, or even Africa-based terrorist networks rather than to anything in Afghanistan.

Some senior European diplomats are painfully aware of the damage that has been done by the Afghan war to the Atlantic Alliance, first by Washington's refusal to involve NATO in the military campaign to topple the Taliban; then by Washington's initial unwillingness to link ISAF to NATO; then by the perceived bait and switch in which Washington, reversing its position more than a year later, invited NATO to perform a peacekeeping role that quickly expanded into a counterinsurgency campaign; then by the European failure to follow through on agreed tasks, such as training the Afghan National Police; then by unilateral American counterterrorist operations; then by restrictive European caveats on troop usage that drove several ISAF commanders to distraction; and, finally, by the accelerated departure schedules of most European coalition partners.

Mutual recriminations related to this damage have been frequently aired and will likely continue to surface as the Americans are progressively left to do the serious fighting. Damage to the NATO alliance is a sunk cost, and there is only so much a peace agreement can do to repair the damage. On the other hand, NATO will certainly be more harmed by a perception of defeat than by an outcome that can be defended as something short of defeat.

European governments and their publics support a peace process for Afghanistan but are not likely to allow it to affect the pace of their military withdrawals. European interests and objectives in Afghanistan thus include, roughly in this order,

- the withdrawal of European combat forces (with minimal bloodshed) on an early timetable
- preventing Al Qaeda and other terrorist franchises from using Afghanistan as a sanctuary
- preserving Afghanistan as a democracy with basic human rights, especially gender rights
- limiting narcotics exports from Afghanistan to Europe.

European governments will insist on provisions that address all of these objectives in any accord to which they are party, but only the first is a true "must have" in the sense that Europeans will achieve it with or without an accord. Most European governments feel that their own domestic vulnerability to terrorist strikes is far more dependent on events in Pakistan and on homegrown cells than from anything planned or organized in Afghanistan. The British in particular perceive the main show to be in Pakistan, and the British security services depend to a significant extent on ISI cooperation in tracking terrorist networks within the large Pakistani Diaspora resident in the United Kingdom.

Summary

Figure 3.1 illustrates the views of the main stakeholders on the issues likely to be at the center of any Afghan peace process. It distinguishes among nine external actors and the following three Afghan parties: the Kabul government, the Taliban, and the legal opposition to the Karzai government (which includes elements of the former Northern Alliance and of current civil society). The issues are withdrawal of

NATO forces, the residual commitments and arrangements to combat terrorism, a commitment by the Afghan parties not to allow their territory to be used against any third party (nonalignment), the reciprocal commitment by Afghanistan's neighbors not to allow their territories to be used to destabilize Afghanistan (noninterference), a promise of continuing American security assistance, a United Nations peacekeeping operation, a commitment by Afghanistan and its neighbors to cooperate against drug trafficking, arrangements for power sharing among the Afghan factions, the role of Islam and sharia law, and commitments by the international community to continue economic assistance to Afghanistan.

Figure 3.1
Stakeholder Views About Issues Central to the Peace Process

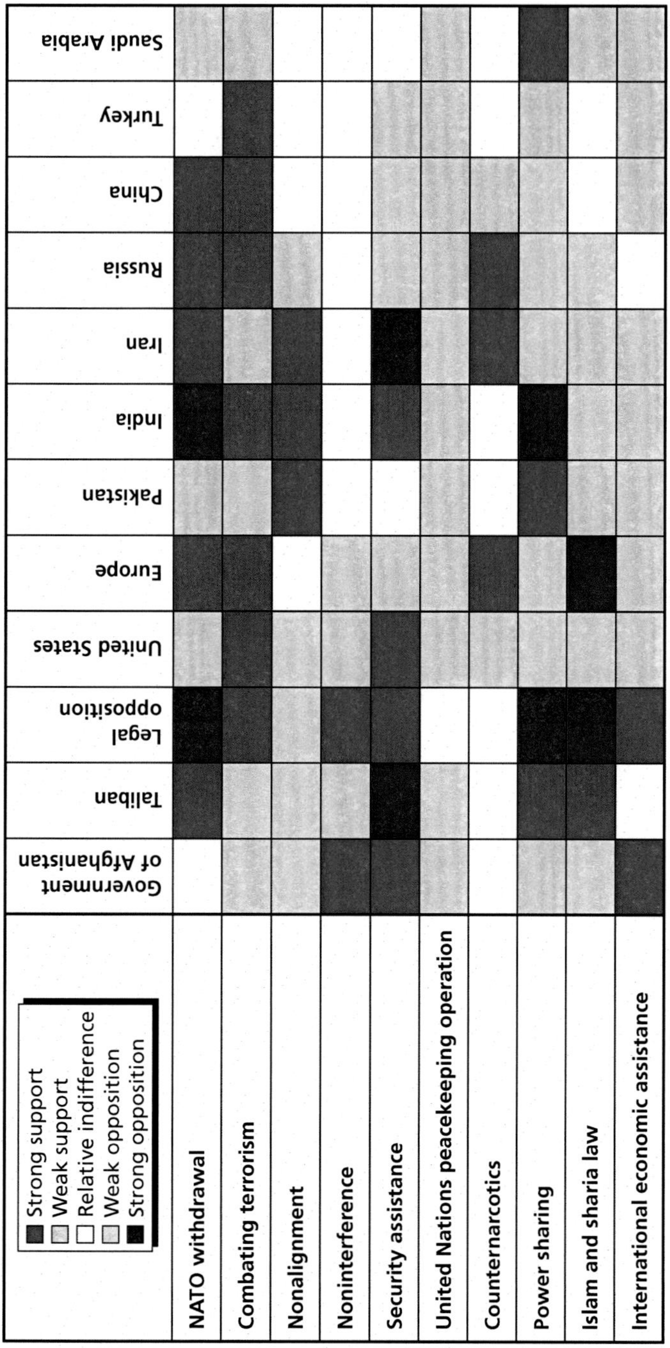

Legend:
- Strong support
- Weak support
- Relative indifference
- Weak opposition
- Strong opposition

Stakeholders (columns): Government of Afghanistan, Taliban, Legal opposition, United States, Europe, Pakistan, India, Iran, Russia, China, Turkey, Saudi Arabia

Issues (rows):
- NATO withdrawal
- Combating terrorism
- Nonalignment
- Noninterference
- Security assistance
- United Nations peacekeeping operation
- Counternarcotics
- Power sharing
- Islam and sharia law
- International economic assistance

RAND *MG1131-3.1*

CHAPTER FOUR

From Discussion to Negotiation to Implementation

Any peace process must pass through three broad stages: first, talking about talks; then, actually negotiating; and, finally, trying to implement the results. The process gets harder, and the risks greater, as it progresses. Those looking forward to the champagne moment of signature in an Afghan peace accord should prepare for a long, hard slog before arriving at that point, and an even harder one thereafter in seeking to implement the undertakings.

The first stage has already begun. The Afghan, American, NATO, and Pakistani governments have endorsed the idea of negotiations with the insurgent leadership. President Karzai has created a High Peace Council, led by former Northern Alliance President Berhanuddin Rabbani, who preceded President Karzai as Afghan head of state. President Karzai has also employed members of his family and his inner circle, including his deputy national security adviser, Engineer Spinzada, to establish contacts and engage in sporadic discussions with insurgent representatives.

Ministers and heads of government have, at NATO and other international gatherings, declared in favor of a peace process. Secretary Clinton has spoken favorably and rather precisely on the topic.[1] The Pakistani military leadership has offered to mediate between President Karzai and the Taliban, although it did send mixed signals by arresting Mullah Beradar, a top deputy of Mullah Omar reputed to be interested

---

[1] In, for example, the aforementioned February 18, 2011, speech to the Asia Society.

in opening talks with Kabul. Saudi Arabia has arranged talks between Afghan government and insurgent representatives, most prominently at an *iftar* in Mecca in 2008. The Taliban leadership has been more circumspect, but various indirect spokespersons and go-betweens have expressed an interest in talks and have outlined the likely insurgent demands in any such negotiation. News reports suggest that American officials have held several conversations in Doha, arranged by the Qatari and German governments, with Taliban figures connected to Mullah Omar. There is, in short, already much talking across the lines.

However, a number of issues remain to be worked out before proceeding to the second stage, actual negotiations. First, who would participate? Second, where would talks take place? Third, under whose auspices? Fourth, what would be the agreed purpose of and agenda for these talks?

Participation

At the center of the process would, of course, be the main Afghan protagonists. However, this means more than someone representing President Karzai and someone else representing Mullah Omar or the Quetta Shura leadership. As our discussion of potential spoilers pointed out, there are several important Afghan constituencies that have the power to subvert any agreement and must therefore be represented in some measure. On the government side are President Karzai's main political foes (some of whom represent the non-Pashtun communities) and civil society (notably, women). These are the elements most likely to oppose any peace with the insurgency if their interests are not accommodated. President Karzai's political rivals might do so forcefully, while civil society would seek bring its influence to bear largely through the international community.

On the insurgent side, the inclusion of the autonomous networks headed by Jalaluddin Haqqani and his son Sirajuddin Haqqani, and of the network led by Gulbuddin Hekmatyar, would also be necessary to assure a comprehensive peace, although it might prove possible to proceed without them initially, if necessary.

Most of the insurgent leaders and much of their support structure is located in Pakistan. The insurgents depend on Pakistan not just for sanctuary but for other forms of material help and advice and for rest, recuperation, and recruitment. It is unlikely that they would or could make peace without the concurrence of the Pakistani military leadership. Furthermore, no agreement could be implemented and enforced without Pakistan's collaboration. Thus, Pakistan's participation in some form in any peace process is essential.

But even that would not be enough. India, Iran, and Russia supported the anti-Taliban resistance prior to 9/11 and would likely do so again if excluded from a Pakistan-brokered peace process, particularly one that left their traditional Hazara, Tajik, and Uzbek clients unhappy. So, these countries must be included in the process in some fashion as well.

The United States and its ISAF coalition allies are obviously central parties to the war. The future presence or absence of foreign military and intelligence forces will be one of the main issues at the heart of any peace negotiation, so these countries need to be represented. And, finally, there is the wider circle of countries, including China, Saudi Arabia, and Turkey as well as the Central Asian republics on Afghanistan's northern borders (Turkmenistan, Tajikistan, and Uzbekistan). These countries could be expected to contribute economically to sustaining any peace settlement and, accordingly, should be given some role in its elaboration. Although only the Afghan parties should participate formally in negotiations about the issues central to their country's future, some role and access needs to be arranged for all the major external stakeholders. If they are excluded from the process, these governments will certainly become spoilers. If they are included and engaged, there is some prospect that they may be persuaded to exercise convergent influence on the Afghan parties.

Location

Security, ease of access, and neutrality are the three criteria for chosing a location. Insurgent representatives are not going to feel safe anywhere in Afghanistan. The insurgents with whom we spoke are very reluctant to negotiate inside Pakistan, and no other party would regard that country as either a secure or neutral locale. Saudi Arabia, one of the smaller Persian Gulf states, such as Qatar, and Turkey are possibilities, although Iran and elements of the legal Afghan opposition would probably object to Saudi Arabia, and Turkey, a combatant as part of the ISAF coalition, may be unacceptable to some of the insurgents. The Germans would certainly like to host such a conference, perhaps even at the same site as the 2001 Bonn Conference. If the Taliban objects to a NATO locale, Geneva is a neutral site combining most of the above attributes. The main disadvantage of Geneva is that, although the host government is certainly neutral, it would also be entirely passive, whereas the Saudi or Turkish governments would probably lend their weight to any effort to broker a settlement and to help implement it over time. Qatar obviously would have less weight than either of these two, but it would still play a more activist and probably more helpful role than the government of Switzerland.

Agenda

The main topics for negotiation among the Afghan parties at the core of the negotiations will be security arrangements, acceptance of the Taliban as a legitimate political force, distribution of power and patronage, constitutional revision, the role of Islam in government and law, and the presence of foreign forces.

In parallel, there will also need to be discussions between the Afghans and their neighbors about the latter's role in sustaining peace and denying support or sanctuary to spoiler elements. There will also need to be talks between the Afghans and the broader international community about the levels of external economic, political, and perhaps even military support that the international community is prepared to provide in the context of an agreement.

A Three-Ring Circus

These considerations suggest the need for a multilayered process with the Afghan parties at the center and surrounded by several wider circles: the first consisting of the United States and Pakistan; the second of India, Iran, and Russia; and the third involving other ISAF troop contributors and large financial donors. These distinctions need not, and as a practical matter cannot, be formalized. India, Iran, and Russia would never agree to be consigned to the second circle, and Saudi Arabia, Turkey, and the United Kingdom would never agree to be placed in the third. And, indeed, participation would need to vary from issue to issue.

However, the essentially Afghan nature of the process will need to be preserved, and confidentiality protected, to the extent possible. Thus, some "need-to-participate" criteria will have to be imposed from one matter to the next. As a retired Pakistani retired general told us, "A peace accord must be an intra-Afghan settlement above all—they [the Afghans] are skillful at playing all outsiders, including you and us."

The outsiders will be wise to avoid being "played," but they will also have to know when to exert pressure, dangle incentives, or withhold support in order to keep the Afghan core participants engaged in serious negotiations and, even more important, committed to actually implementing the conditions so concluded.

The Need for a Ringmaster

Someone will need to convene, host, and preside over such a process. History provides a number of possible models.

Private groups have on occasion mediated peace settlements. For example, the Center for Humanitarian Dialogue (formerly the Henri Dunant Foundation) played a key role facilitating the peace accord between the Indonesian government and the Gerakan Aceh Merdeka insurgency in Sumatra. The UN has mediated peace settlements more frequently than have private groups, and, from time to time, regional organizations (such as the African Union or Arab League) have served in this role.

Sometimes a national government has convened, hosted, and presided over such a process, as the United States did in the Bosnian peace negotiations in 1995. More rarely, the protagonists themselves have taken charge and engaged without the benefit of third-party facilitation, as the United States and North Vietnam did in 1968, with France providing the venue but playing no other role in the talks.

It seems unlikely that the Afghan government and the Taliban leadership, left to their own devices, would be capable of orchestrating the sort of multilayered process described earlier. A single government could act as both host and ringmaster, but this would require a very unusual, probably in this case unattainable, combination of impartiality, commitment, and capacity for skillful diplomacy.

In the absence of a single organization that can fill all three of these requirements, it may be necessary to identify both an impartial host that offers a secure and accessible site and a separate convening and presiding authority with the requisite impartiality and diplomatic capacity. The best combination would be a UN-endorsed facilitator known and trusted by the main parties, particularly the United States, and a Western site, perhaps in Qatar, Turkey, or Germany (Geneva would be an acceptable alternative).

From Talks to Negotiations

Securing agreement on the conditions for talks, including participation, location, convenor, and agenda, will not be easy, given the differing views and interests of the essential parties outlined in the preceding chapter. At present, no one has responsibility for brokering such a procedural accord, and there seems, accordingly, to have been no real progress in the move from the exploratory talks to real negotiations. President Karzai and insurgent Taliban figures have thus far engaged in rather desultory and inconclusive contacts, some facilitated by Saudi Arabia. American, British, and UN officials have done the same, putting out feelers and searching for a credible interlocutor. Pakistan is clearly in contact with both sides and at multiple levels. These exchanges seem unlikely to coalesce into real negotiations any time soon, however, given the mistrust among all those so engaged, the low level of coherence in the objectives of most of the players, and the limited capacity to put together such a complex, multitiered diplomatic process.

The United States has that capacity, but an American effort to take a visible lead in advancing negotiations may overshadow the Afghan government and diminish Kabul's bargaining leverage once talks are under way. Moreover, an urgent American effort to convene peace negotiations is likely to be interpreted as a sign of weakness and thus to prolong the war, rather than end it. Finally, as one of the major combatants, the United States is not well placed to mediate even a procedural accord.

Thus, just as the formal negotiation itself will probably need an impartial and diplomatically adroit facilitator, a neutral and competent person will be essential to putting together the procedural accord that must precede any substantive talks. The Century Foundation report described at some length the qualifications and mandate of such a facilitator and how he or she might interface with the United Nations.[2]

Structuring the Formal Negotiations

Neither the United States nor any of the other interested governments need directly participate in the intra-Afghan dialogue. But they will want to keep a close eye on its progress. All of these governments will undoubtedly send delegations to wherever the Afghan peace talks take place. There, they will be able interact with each other and with the various Afghan participants. The host and the convener of these negotiations (not necessarily the same entity) should work to both preserve the essentially Afghan nature of the talks and provide other interested and influential governments with access to the negotiating parties.

---

[2]   The Century Foundation, 2011, pp. 50–53.

Obviously, American officials will consult closely with the Kabul government on its negotiating tactics, but they should also be active in persuading other parties to put convergent pressures on all the Afghan participants. Arms must be twisted and incentives proffered at the right time and in a coordinated fashion, or at least as coordinated as can be expected, given the varying priorities of the various external parties. This is complex diplomatic music to orchestrate.

In parallel with talks among the Afghan parties, the neighbors and other interested governments on the fringes of this formal process should discuss steps they could take in common to support and sustain a peace accord. Such steps could include political, military, and economic measures. Politically, for example, neighboring states could pledge not to allow their territory to be used by opponents of a peace accord. Militarily, the broader international community might want to consider the composition of a peacekeeping force that could replace ISAF and oversee implementation of a peace agreement. Economically, neighboring states could consider free trade or other commercial agreements, and the larger international community could prepare pledges of development assistance and funding for the demobilization and reintegration of combatants from both sides.

At some stage, it will make sense to convene a larger international gathering where an intra-Afghan accord can be both endorsed and embedded in a series of wider multilateral commitments along the above lines. This would be the champagne moment so beloved by statesmen. Moving to such a formal multilateral process should depend, however, on first achieving substantial progress in the negotiations between the Afghan parties. This would allow a more or less united and representative Afghan delegation to take part in such talks and enter into the resultant commitments.

Implementation

The history of peace accords between undefeated opponents is not encouraging. Any such accord requires both sides to engage in some considerable degree of disarmament. Fear of betrayal often causes one side or both to balk at such a step. Unless there is an impartial third party, trusted by both sides and capable of overseeing implementation, the lack of mutual confidence between the former enemies often causes implementation to falter and conflict to be renewed. Recent Afghan history has more than its share of failed cease-fires and peace agreements.

A successful Afghan peace agreement will contain both political and military provisions, and it will entail significant expenses, most of which will have to be borne by external parties. Among the political provisions are likely to be alterations to the existing constitution, new elections, and the appointment of new officials. Among the economic expenses will be the costs of disarming, demobilizing, and reintegrating combatants from both sides. Indeed, given the large size of the Afghan government's current armed forces relative to the number of insurgents, the cost of scaling back the government forces to peacetime levels will greatly exceed the costs of demobilizing the insurgents. As noted, it will probably be essential for some neutral third party to monitor these processes and cajole the Afghans into fulfilling their promises and implementing the accord as negotiated.

The United States and NATO, as major combatants, will probably not be in a position to provide this kind of impartial oversight. Furthermore, neither Afghan party is likely to want any of Afghanistan's neighbors playing such a role. There will thus be a need for some more neutral party, perhaps the UN, to organize a peacekeeping force. The task of this peacekeeping force will not be to compel implementation but rather to fill the likely interim security vacuum created as Western forces withdraw and to reassure all parties that they can safely fulfill the pledges they have made to disarm and share power.

CHAPTER FIVE

The Terms of a Peace Accord

The terms of any peace accord will likely involve a ceasefire and a release of prisoners from both sides, the removal of most Taliban leaders from the UN's blacklist, a schedule for withdrawing ISAF from Afghanistan, the severing of the insurgency's links with Al Qaeda, the "sharia-ization" of some elements of governance and some parts of the country, assurances for former members of the Northern Alliance, administrative decentralization, and political participation by the Taliban in the government of Afghanistan as a minority partner in a coalition (including some power sharing at the district and provincial levels). An accord among the Afghan parties to the current conflict along these lines would likely be accompanied by a related, but perhaps separate, agreement between its neighbors and other external parties in which the former commit to certain positive and negative undertakings designed to stabilize Afghanistan and secure the peace.

Security

As Chapter Three shows, security issues account for two-thirds of the objectives of the various actors involved in an Afghan peace process. All the external parties prize preventing Afghanistan from reverting to a sanctuary for international terrorist networks. All actors seek a withdrawal of Western military forces at some point, the main issues being timing and conditionality. Similarly, most participants would welcome an assurance of Afghan nonalignment.

An interim cease-fire and other limited agreements might cause the wholesale fighting to halt long enough to allow a more comprehensive accord to be cobbled, but some initial confidence-building measures—e.g., safe passage for negotiations, selective prisoner releases on both sides—would likely have to precede a cease-fire. Temporary arrangements to limit hostilities could be negotiated on a national level or worked out on a decentralized basis at a provincial or district level.

One Taliban district commander suggested that

> a sequence of peace would begin with a confidence dialogue, maybe at the local level, maybe in a district that is a peace haven, with a cease-fire and exchange of prisoners. If that worked, it could expand to a cease-fire on a general, countrywide basis. Then would begin the process of withdrawal of ISAF forces and introduction of some peacekeeping forces, with an interim government [of national reconciliation]. Finally we would have a comprehensive political settlement.

The Afghan insurgency is a mosaic of different fighters, grudges, and tribal alliances that vary from place to place. Given some kind of green light from both Kabul and the Quetta Shura, and encouragement and some assurances from both ISAF and Pakistan, a variety of local cease-fires might emerge. According to the same Taliban commander, the Taliban "will not surrender our arms to the Karzai government or to ISAF, but maybe to a 'people's shura,' on a local basis."

The suspension of hostilities may last in some districts but may crumble quickly in others. There are many potential spoilers to a peace process in Afghanistan, and there will be bitter-enders on both sides of the conflict, including hard-line district-level jihadis among the Taliban, who view any accommodation with Kabul and ISAF as a betrayal. Local commanders and local power brokers on government side, who have more to gain from continuing strife than from a peaceful resolution, might also break ranks. All parties seem to agree that security terms need to be put in place quickly as a peace process unfolds. As a senior Hezb-i-Islami political figure associated with Hekmatyar told us, "We don't want a security vacuum, a period of chaos such as in 1992." This sentiment was echoed by a military district commander from the same faction, and it seems to be almost universally shared. Al Qaeda and other small but violent non-Afghan extremist groups, such as the Islamic Movement of Uzbekistan, face an existential threat from any Afghan peace accord; they will declare war on any peace process and seek to derail with violence both negotiations and accord implementation. The high level of residual background violence caused by narcotraffickers and garden-variety criminal gangs in Afghanistan will also threaten any such process. These spoilers have both the manpower and the guns—and the incentive—to undermine peace. Finally, there are the many subtribes and remote valley communities throughout Afghanistan that distrust both the Kabul government and the Taliban, prefer to be left alone, and are prepared to defend their autonomy by force.

The most difficult challenge confronting any peace process in Afghanistan will be establishing and sustaining, despite the many potential spoilers, a minimum of law and order going into and lasting throughout the resultant political transition. It will be important—and difficult—both for the parties to an accord and for international peacekeepers to identify deliberate violations of cease-fires that occur against the country's high level of background violence.

Peace in Afghanistan will require the gradual removal of foreign forces and the disarmament, demobilization, and reintegration (DDR) of three sets of indigenous forces. The latter include the Afghan army and police, the Taliban fighters, and the many private militias maintained by private security firms and other local power brokers. Of these groups, the forces under Taliban control are actually the smallest in number and thus present, from a practical (although not necessarily political) standpoint, the smallest DDR challenge.

Far more difficult, or at least more expensive, will be scaling back the Afghan government's security establishment to sustainable peacetime levels. The Afghan army and police must be expanded and strengthened so that major security control can be handed off progressively to the Afghans between 2011 and 2014. In the event of a peace accord, however, a number of Taliban fighters will need to be integrated into these forces in some fashion and given the task of providing basic law and order despite the depredations of various spoilers. And, as just noted, the entire security establishment will need to be scaled back over time. Afghanistan cannot afford, either financially or politically, to maintain such large armed forces. The reintegration aspect of DDR will be particularly important if demobilization is not to vastly increase the ranks of local bandit militias and common criminals willing to offer themselves to political spoilers, narcotraffickers, recalcitrant Taliban commanders, and unhappy warlords.

An effective new DDR process will depend on several variables, including the level of security attained in most parts of the country (given the high residual background violence in Afghanistan); the scale of activity and violence perpetrated by narcotics traffickers; how major warlords and other local strongmen are prosecuted, amnestied, exiled, or (more likely) co-opted into the new arrangements; and the nature of logistics arrangements associated with the phased NATO withdrawal, which will, in turn, affect the cash flow of private security companies and even Taliban groups that are paid not to disrupt NATO supply convoys. The Afghan National Police presents a particularly delicate problem, for although its members are locally drawn and therefore more reflective of local ethnic balances at the grassroots level, the organization is widely regarded as corrupt and predatory. However, the police are integral to the local patron-client networks against whom the Taliban is, for local reasons, fighting.

The United States and its allies will need to support a negotiation process while fighting a war and continuing to prepare Afghan soldiers and police to assume greater responsibilities. The areas under the effective control of the Kabul government must be consolidated, protected, and expanded in order to keep the Taliban at the negotiating table. In addition, pressure on the Taliban leadership must be maintained through intelligence and special operations forces activities; however, their rules of engagement must be adapted to enable ongoing negotiations (e.g., they must support local cease-fires and other confidence-building measures). It is never easy to use combat operations to shape a political process, but that is precisely what any Afghan peace process will require.

Adapting combat operations to negotiating necessities will raise numerous issues. Who is a legitimate representative of the Taliban and its associated networks, or of the Kabul government? What constitutes a "safe area" for negotiations? How long will it be "safe"? How can safe passage for insurgent representatives to and from such talks be reasonably guaranteed? What happens if a bona fide negotiator is wounded, killed, or captured, whether by either side or a spoiler? Confidence-building measures will need to be designed and mutually agreed to address these sorts of issues.

As noted, all of the participants in an Afghan peace process other than India favor the withdrawal of Western militaries. The difficult terms to hammer out in this regard include the timing of the withdrawal, the conditions that will have to be met before their departure, and what, if any, components will remain to help train and enable residual Afghan national forces.

The Kabul regime is likely to prefer a slow withdrawal of NATO forces and some limited residual American military presence. The Taliban, conversely, prefers the immediate and total withdrawal and will likely oppose any continued military training and supply activities conducted by Western militaries unless those activities are carefully controlled by a new Kabul regime that includes Taliban participation. Neighboring governments prefer that ISAF withdraws sooner rather than later, though not at the risk of creating a vacuum that other neighbors or terrorist groups might fill. Western governments prefer a phased withdrawal with a clear timeline. The United States is likely to seek a continued intelligence and special operations forces presence, and this, along with Taliban ties to Al Qaeda, is likely to be among the last sticking points in any negotiation.

Another important and difficult issue will be what foreign peace-keeping forces, if any, replace ISAF. Experience in conflict termination elsewhere has demonstrated that peace accords tend to break down rather quickly in the absence of some third-party oversight because the contending parties do not trust each other sufficiently to implement the provisions to which they have agreed, particularly provisions that relate to disarmament and power sharing. It is hard to imagine an Afghan accord being carried out successfully without some degree of third-party monitoring, arbitration, and adjudication. A residual peacekeeping force need not be strong enough to compel adherence by a clearly unwilling party (something even American and NATO forces have been unable to accomplish), but it would need to be robust enough to help ensure that lower-level operatives on either side obey higher-level guidance from their respective leaderships and to make any circumvention of the accord difficult and therefore obvious. Such a force will need to be authorized to use force in pursuit of its mission, but it should not be expected to coerce the major parties to the peace accord.

Both the Kabul government and the Taliban will probably accept some non-Western peacekeeping force for a limited period. The size, composition, mandate, and direction of such a force will be matters for negotiation. The most likely outcome is a UN-led peacekeeping force largely made up of non-Western troop contingents from countries that do not border Afghanistan. At least some of these contingents might come from more-distant Islamic countries, such as Indonesia, Jordan, and Malaysia. Turkey might also be an acceptable participant, despite its NATO membership and participation in ISAF. None of these countries would agree to dispatch troops, however, without some convincing promises from all parties to the conflict that they will honor the agreement and respect the peacekeeping force. They will also be seriously concerned about the possibility of terrorist attacks on peacekeeping forces by Al Qaeda or the many potential spoilers to a peace accord. Counterterrorism is not normally a task for which peacekeeping forces are trained or equipped, and a mission to Afghanistan would probably break new ground in that respect. The need to provide counterterrorism intelligence and strike forces for a UN peacekeeping operation may, for Afghans, provide a face-saving and politically palatable way to maintain a residual American counterterrorist presence after an accord.

Governance

Although external participants may have opinions and advice about Afghanistan's system of government, this is, at the end of the day, something the Afghans themselves will have to sort out. In doing so, they will draw primarily on their own history and experience and will pay scant attention to outside advice.

Afghans are wary, for instance, of federalism, which they fear could irremediably rupture their weak state and fragmented society. Yet, any durable power-sharing arrangement will require some modification to the existing highly centralized presidential system, which has few checks and balances. What form could a power-sharing agreement hammered out between the IEA and the Government of the Islamic Republic of Afghanistan take? How legitimate would the result be considered by the Afghan people? How would this agreement be reflected in constitutional and institutional terms?

As Chapter Three indicated, three of the top four objectives of both the Taliban and the Kabul regime relate to the manner in which a government of national reconciliation is structured. Western governments and, significantly, Iran will want to ensure that any such arrangements provide sufficient guarantees of inclusion and protection to the country's non-Pashtun minorities and, in the case of Western governments, women. But, at the end of the day, these questions will be decided largely by the Afghans themselves.

The domain for power-sharing arrangements includes the national, regional, and local levels. The process might go forward in two phases, beginning with some sort of interim "government of national reconciliation" at the top and leaving most of the more fundamental political questions for future resolution in a second phase. Detailed rules about structure, elections, and so forth could be resolved by a *loya jirga* [constitutional convention] and ultimately lead to a plebiscite on a modified constitution. Alternatively, an accord might specify constitutional changes that would need to be implemented before some other elements of the agreement (disarmament, for instance) could come into force. It is even possible, although less likely, that the Afghan parties might agree to an entirely new constitutional arrangement. Changes to the current constitution, if they are approved by the Kabul regime and the Taliban and supported by the international community, could probably be incorporated through the mechanisms set out in the existing document.

Afghan governments have always been formally centralized, but this has traditionally been counterbalanced by strong, if informal, local institutions based on tribal and communal affiliations. Remnants of these traditional structures remain but have been damaged and distorted by three decades of warfare. The current Afghan government is not only centralized but also dominated by its elected President, who appoints all senior national officials and local governors. He also exercises influence through relatives and other local power brokers. The Kabul regime can thus be viewed as a complex patchwork of vertical patron-client relations, many (but not all) of which feed upward, ultimately, to the Presidential Palace. Governance of this type is common in many traditional, premodern, or tribal nations and in countries with relatively weak institutional structures.

Conceivably, the Taliban might come to favor a more decentralized model of governance that would leave its officials in control of significant areas of the country, with their tenure not subject to the whim of the incumbent President. This would be quite contrary to the Taliban's own practice while in power and to its theologically derived views on the role of the state. The IEA had no constitution, instead relying for its authority on the Quran and sharia law and on personal links and oaths of fealty to Mullah Omar. The resultant government was at least as centralized as today's, although much less formalized. Some reports suggest that Pashtuns in the east of the country are more open to decentralized structures than those in the Taliban heartland of Kandahar and Helmand.

On the issue of central versus local power, there is likely to be a set of fluid coalitions on both sides of the issue within both the Kabul regime and the Taliban. Some in the Taliban may make common cause with conservative elements within the Kabul coalition (e.g., with Hezb-i-Islami).[1] Civil society representatives and the legal opposition in Kabul will have strongly felt views on these issues.

---

[1] Giustozzi (2010, p. 13) writes,

> At least for a phase, a settlement achieved in the presence of an ascendant Taliban would have to include a coalition government with Taliban participation. Such a coalition would be unlikely to be all inclusive, or even widely inclusive. In fact it is difficult to see

"Everyone is looking for where they will sit—or go into exile—after a peace settlement," observed one Western diplomat. When the harsh music of war grinds to a stop, all the main contenders will expect some place to sit. Those who have none will be faced with the options of fighting on as bitter-enders, fading into the background (with dim prospects), going into exile in Dubai or Pakistan, or possibly going to jail. External governments may need to discreetly provide some of these figures with asylum, side payments, and guarantees of amnesty, whether formal or informal, in order to encourage a settlement.

For example, the Turks might invite General Dostum to renew his residence in Bodrum, the Saudis could invite Mullah Omar to retire to Mecca, Iran might invite Ismail Khan to take up genteel residence in Mashad, and so forth. It would be an important task for any facilitator of a peace process to discreetly sound out the retirement intentions of domestic Afghan figures, especially the likely spoilers, and explore the welcome mat that external powers might extend to them. As cautioned earlier, one element that will certainly not be present in any likely Afghan peace accord is effective and enforceable provisions for war crimes tribunals or other forms of transitional justice. No Afghan human rights organizations are currently seeking such arrangements, and they will probably instead focus on excluding some of the worst offenders from public office.

A government of national reconciliation in Kabul could establish new provincial and district shura made up of a balanced set of representatives from both sides in the current conflict. With the objective of gradually integrating government and Taliban patron-client networks,

---

how it would be possible to have a functioning government which included representatives of all factions, ranging from the secular progressive to the Taliban. The Taliban would probably try to maneuver and form a more restrictive coalition, incorporating like-minded groups (i.e., Islamic fundamentalist and Islamist groups). Even that might not lead to a very functional government, given the gap between the abilities of the likely partners in the coalition and the administrative demands that the system established in Afghanistan after 2001 imposes. Such a government would probably also not be very representative of the different regions and ethnic groups and sects, not to mention gender. However, considering that the present government is not very functional either, nor necessarily very representative, it still might be seen as an acceptable option both internally and externally as long as it brings the war to an end.

it could then accord these councils more authority over local governance (including police, justice, and access to tax resources) than the existing councils currently enjoy. It would be only reasonable to expect a high degree of local variation in these arrangements that is based on history, tribal alignments, traditional blood feuds, and the military balance of power between progovernment and pro-Taliban forces prior to an accord.[2]

As part of any power-sharing deal, it will be helpful to have some agreed mechanisms for dealing with the murder or abduction of shura members from either side and to establish methods for distinguishing between unfortunate accidents attributable to Afghanistan's background violence and deliberate attempts by either side to undermine the peace agreement.

Belgium, Bosnia, Iraq, and Lebanon offer models of formal and informal arrangements for power sharing among competing sectarian groups. None of these countries is terribly well governed, but neither is any currently experiencing civil war. As part of this evolution, the Afghans might choose to move from a presidential to parliamentary system, perhaps chosen via proportional representation. This would avoid the winner-take-all nature of the current arrangement, in which, as noted earlier, the popularly elected President fills all other senior posts. It would also force the contending factions into multiparty coali-

---

[2]   As one analyst writes,

> A political system based on a wider set of patronage links would build on the patchwork of regional and local power structures that already operate in Afghanistan, as well as the country's history of decentralized governance. Kabul would delegate authority to governors to run their domains with substantial autonomy from the central government, according to political arrangements that might take different forms in different parts of the country. A power-sharing arrangement based on asymmetrical devolution would have to include not just the Taliban but be part of a broader Afghanistan-wide political settlement. Those currently benefitting from access to patronage have a vested interest in not allowing others in. However, were it not for the international military presence that has shielded Karzai's government and personal networks from having to share power, deal-making of this nature would probably already have happened between Afghan elites. (Minna Järvenpää, "A Political Settlement in Afghanistan: Preparing for the Long Game, Not the Endgame," in Wolfgang Danspeckgruber, ed., *Working Toward Peace and Prosperity in Afghanistan*, Boulder, Colo.: Lynne Rienner Press, July 2010, p. 9)

tions in order to govern, since no faction, and certainly not the Taliban, could win half or more of the seats.

In a discussion with the authors, a former Northern Alliance leader predicted that,

> once negotiations start, there will be lots of changes in [our] constitution, demanded by all sides. We [the former Northern Alliance groups] will demand decentralization guarantees so that a government with Taliban participation won't become a dominant Pashtun government squeezing us. The Karzai government needs to reconcile with us as well as reconcile with [the] Taliban.

The Kabul government has held several elections. The last two were flawed, but the regime nevertheless has far more democratic legitimacy than any of its neighbors, with the possible exception of Pakistan. The Taliban originally seized national power by force, was never subject to a popular election, was widely discredited by its harsh rule between 1996 and 2001, and currently enjoys the support of no more than about 10 percent of the population. (This support is heavily concentrated in the south and east of the country.) It has achieved credibility in some areas under its control by administering rough sharia justice, but it has offered no other public services. The Afghan population longs for peace, supports peace talks, and is likely, in large measure, to give any new government that emerges from such a process an opportunity to prove itself.

All external parties to an Afghan peace process want to see a stable, friendly government in Kabul, but some of them equate "friendly to them" with "hostile to their adversaries." None of the external parties wants to see the return of a Taliban-dominated Islamic emirate. Pakistan and Saudi Arabia had close relationships with the Taliban and were quick to grant diplomatic recognition to the IEA in 1996, but neither government wants a return to the situation that produced 9/11. Pakistan and Saudi Arabia will favor enough Taliban participation in a national unity government to end the war and get the Taliban out of Pakistan. India and Iran, on the other hand, will want to minimize Taliban influence in any resultant government. China and Russia will also want to limit American influence over that government.

Western governments will want to ensure that any new system of government is based on democratic norms and respectful human rights, those of women in particular. Several Taliban and former Taliban interlocutors told us that Taliban leaders recognize that the organization cannot revert to some of its earlier social practices. These leaders' assertions must be regarded with considerable skepticism. Nevertheless, Afghans will not easily give up the social and economic gains they have made since 2001. Women's education, for instance, is quite popular throughout the country, and the Taliban leadership have had to restrain local commanders from targeting such facilities. Resistance to the reintroduction of fundamentalist social norms at a national level would likely be quite strong, but there could be greater toleration for localized variances in practice. There already exists throughout the country considerable variance in social practices, with women and minorities enjoying far more freedom in large urban centers than in some more-conservative rural ones. This lack of uniformity would likely increase under any government emerging from a peace accord, particularly if it devolves authority downward.

Terrorism

As a former Taliban minister told us, "Our ties with Al Qaeda will end with a negotiated peace accord. Our alliance with Al Qaeda is a fighting alliance, a convenience of war." Washington and other participants will insist that the Taliban provide credible assurances that its cooperation with international terrorist networks will be terminated. Verification will require extensive surveillance and intelligence monitoring from outside and may result in some residual American counterterrorism intelligence and strike capability remaining inside Afghanistan, although that may be hard to achieve.

In the long run, counterterrorism operations in Afghanistan will have to shift toward Afghan-led efforts and away from reliance on military force. It is important for the durability of any peace accord that suspected terrorists be arrested and incarcerated by Afghan forces rather than dealt with by American drone strikes or night raids, which can leave innocent casualties in their wake. The Indonesian government (admittedly a far more capable and coherent government than Afghanistan's) had remarkable success with its law enforcement approach to dismantling the Al Qaeda–affiliated Jemaah Islamiya terrorist movement between 2002 and 2008.

The sine qua non of an acceptable agreement for the United States and its allies is total rupture between the Taliban and Al Qaeda, while the comparable demand from the Taliban is the departure of Western forces. It is likely that each side will withhold what the other wants until the last moment. For the United States and the international community at large, there is, nevertheless, a real danger in pursuing a symmetrical trade-off between these two terms. It would be far easier for the Taliban to verify the removal of hundreds of thousands of uniformed foreign soldiers under formal command structures than for the United States and its allies to monitor the disarmament of hundreds of foreign terrorists in clandestine networks who are "swimming in the sea" of the Afghan people. Nevertheless, there will be an early opportunity to test Taliban intentions in this regard, as any acceptable accord will certainly require that it either turn over or at least reveal the location of all remaining Al Qaeda elements either operating in Afghanistan or hiding in Taliban-dominated areas of Pakistan.

Al Qaeda is terrorist enemy number one for the United States, for some Western European countries, and perhaps for Saudi Arabia. However, other countries feel most threatened by other groups: China by the East Turkestan Islamic Movement, India by Lashkar-e-Taiba, Iran by the Jundallah, Pakistan by the TTP, Russia by the Chechens, and Turkey by the Kurdistan Workers' Party. Pakistan stands the most to gain immediately if the Afghan Taliban and the Pakistan Taliban are pulled apart. Each these governments will be more concerned that any peace accord severs ties between the Taliban and the particular insurgency of concern than between the Taliban and Al Qaeda, and they might seek to block any accord that fails to do so.

We do not know to what degree general concerns about terrorist activities may offset the desire of all Afghan and neighboring parties to see American forces withdraw entirely. It is possible that an accord might contain some general language endorsing continued assistance to the resultant Afghan government in the areas of counterterrorism and counternarcotics. It remains to be seen how much the Taliban and the neighboring governments would find even a watered-down, residual counterterrorism presence acceptable. Among state actors, Iran and Pakistan have the most conflicted position on this issue, since both states employ state-sponsored terrorism as a foreign policy tool. This will not prevent them from joining in general condemnation of such behavior (since they deny their own complicity), but it would reduce the credibility of any commitments they might take in this regard.

Pakistan's position on these issues will depend on which competing narrative proves to more accurately reflect Islamabad's intentions. It is possible that, as a former Pakistani general told us and as noted earlier, "Pakistan's military leadership has gotten the message that they are now in the gun sights of the jihadis, that the real risk to them is here in Western Pakistan, not from the Indians." This would, however, represent a massive and fundamental shift in traditional Pakistani priorities.

Narcotics

Illicit revenues from narcotics are likely to outstrip all other sources of funds in postconflict Afghanistan. A peace accord will not meaningfully curb Afghanistan's narcotics exports but should seek to address the drug trade, which fuels the civil conflict. Traffickers are likely to thrive in the "grey area" between the initial cessation of wholesale warfare and the time-consuming efforts of a coalition government to establish the basic rule of law (including a counternarcotics component) around the country. They will have every incentive, and quite a few means, to disrupt this peace and the expansion of governance and law enforcement. They are natural-born spoilers: brutal, heavily armed, and ruthless.

Counternarcotics is an objective of most external actors, although it is only a "nice to have" for all parties other than Russia (and, even for Russia, it is low on the list). Counternarcotics is also notably absent from the top objectives of both the Taliban and the Kabul government. As with counterterrorism, this means that external parties will have to insist that the issue be dealt with in any peace accord, and they will need to be ready to promise resources to support positive assurances from the Afghan parties to deal with illicit drugs in the future. This suggests that counternarcotics will get largely rhetorical treatment in the terms of an Afghanistan peace accord, despite the risk that traffickers will cause a great deal of background violence as an accord is implemented. As an Afghan businessman suggested to one of us, not entirely in jest, this risk could be ameliorated by appointing a hard-line Taliban mullah as the Minister of Counternarcotics in the power-sharing terms of a government of national reconciliation.

Trade and Investment

Despite its importance to Afghanistan's long-term economic growth, the volume of trade with and investment in Afghanistan is currently far too small to support the complex process of demobilization, political accommodation, and reshuffling of patron-client networks required for successful execution of a peace accord. At bottom, Afghanistan is just too grindingly poor. Top figures in any interim government, whether from the Taliban or the current Kabul regime, will almost certainly make an unseemly grab at the international money flows. The terms of sustained financial and military aid from the international community should be structured to support a decentralized approach to governance but without dictating the terms of that structure—a difficult condition to meet. Aid also needs to be distributed in a fashion that fosters inclusion rather than division among the parties to the new coalition, and it will therefore have to flow to Taliban-dominated areas of the country as well as to areas governed by more-acceptable figures.

The economic terms of any peace accord will have to provide for a continued high level of international economic assistance to Afghanistan once the fighting stops. Equally important is that external donors channel that assistance in ways that support the implementation of an accord rather than ignoring or undermining it. The deep distrust that many donor governments and NGOs currently feel toward the Kabul regime will only worsen as former Taliban figures join a government of national reconciliation. Taliban forces have intimidated, kidnapped, and murdered a number of unarmed aid workers, NGO personnel, and UN employees in Afghanistan. Memories of this violence will not fade quickly.

Expanded trade and investment is a significant, although not dominant, goal for all of Afghanistan's regional partners. Notably, this goal includes trade through and across Afghanistan, creating a bridge between Iran, Central Asia, and South Asia. All parties stand to gain significantly if security of the ring road and border crossings can be assured. Some sort of regional trade liberalization and transit agreement could conceivably be negotiated as part of, or in parallel to, an Afghan peace accord.

Direct investment from China, India, Pakistan, and Iran would be a welcome contributor to the economic recovery of Afghanistan. It would also provide a way to consolidate the commitment of these neighbors to the successful execution of an accord over time.

Positive and Negative Assurances

Any Afghan peace accord is likely to consist of a series of positive and negative assurances offered by both of the Afghan parties and some or all of the external participants.

Potential positive assurances involving active commitments by states to support a peace agreement include the following:

- Neighbors and interested parties agree to guarantee Afghanistan's nonalignment and territorial integrity.
- Afghanistan and Pakistan agree to cooperate in maintaining order on their common border and to submit their border disputes to some form of mediation, arbitration, or adjudication.
- Afghanistan undertakes to form a government of national reconciliation; the UN undertakes to facilitate the formation of this reconciliation government; the neighboring states, the United States, and NATO undertake to recognize and support this new government.

- The United States and NATO agree to a phased withdrawal.
- The UN Security Council agrees to deploy a peacekeeping force to oversee implementation of the peace accord.
- The United States and NATO agree to continue to supply weapons, equipment, and training to the Afghan National Security Forces for a specified period.
- Afghanistan agrees to combat the illicit drug trade, and other governments promise to provide continuing support to this effort.
- Afghanistan agrees to combat international terrorism, and other governments promise to provide continuing support to this effort.
- The international community promises to provide a certain level of economic assistance to Afghanistan over a specified period.

Potential negative assurances involving commitments *not* to take certain actions or to cease doing certain things include the following:

- Afghanistan declares itself to be permanently nonaligned; all parties agree to respect and not seek to undermine that nonalignment.
- Afghanistan undertakes to prevent its territory from being used against the interests of any of its neighbors, and Afghanistan's neighbors undertake to prevent their territory from being used against the interests of Afghanistan.
- Afghanistan undertakes to prevent its territory from being used to harbor terrorist groups or individuals, as defined by the UN Security Council.
- The United States and its NATO allies agree not to redeploy forces into Afghanistan.
- The United States and its NATO allies, along with all of Afghanistan's neighbors, agree not to supply weapons or other material to any parties in Afghanistan other than as may be specified elsewhere in the accord.

These negative assurances are the mirror image of five of the positive assurances in the first list. Promising not to do something is often easier and usually cheaper than promising to do something new. Thus, negative assurances may be more readily achievable. However, the negative assurances identified here are unlikely to be fulfilled in a sustained fashion unless they are backed up by the positive promises on the first list.

CHAPTER SIX

Conclusions and Recommendations

Of all the major participants in any Afghan peace process, the United States will likely feel the greatest sense of urgency. This is because domestic support for the war is waning and because the Obama administration has publicly committed to a timetable for military drawdown. All of the non-Western parties find the current situation—with the United States tied down and neither side able to prevail—tolerable. Indeed, for Iran, the current situation is probably optimal.

Even if Washington feels the greatest sense of urgency, it would be wise not to show as much. Hurried American efforts to jumpstart a negotiation are more likely to dissuade than convince the other parties that the time is ripe to initiate such a process. In any case, the United States, as one of the main protagonists in the struggle, is not in a position to launch and then orchestrate the kind of multitiered process that will be needed to reach a durable Afghan settlement. We therefore recommend that Washington work quietly to secure the nomination, probably by the UN Secretary General, of a figure of international repute with the requisite impartiality, knowledge, contacts, and diplomatic skills to take on the tasks.

We believe that negotiations have a fair chance of succeeding, but we cannot be certain. Thus, American policymakers must also prepare an acceptable, although less attractive, alternative. Ideally, this alternative will be unacceptable, or at least considerably less attractive than a negotiated settlement, to the other parties. Creating such an alternative allows the United States to hedge against failure while simultaneously motivating the other parties to work for success.

American policymakers should, therefore, prepare for two futures: one negotiated, one not. Both must meet the bottom-line need to prevent Afghanistan from falling into the hands of an Al Qaeda–linked regime. This means preparing both to stay indefinitely and to go definitively. If negotiations fail, some level of American military engagement will probably be necessary well beyond the 2014 date by which President Obama has promised to remove all American combat forces. On the other hand, the full withdrawal of American troops from the country is probably a necessary component of any peace deal. Promising to leave is the American counterpart to the Taliban's commitment to cut its ties with Al Qaeda. These concessions represent each side's highest cards and are likely to be played only at the culmination of any negotiating process.

It is thus perfectly reasonable for Washington and Kabul to be negotiating, as they are, the text of a long-term strategic partnership, one with an enduring military component. Indeed, without the prospect of such an enduring American presence, the Taliban would have little incentive to negotiate rather than just wait the United States and NATO out. On the other hand, American and Afghan officials should also be making clear, at least privately, that any such accord between Kabul and Washington would be subject to amendment, depending on the outcome of a peace process.

As the most powerful participant, the United States will have to play a leading but not obviously central role in a complex, multitiered negotiation process. To the extent that an international facilitator can play the public role of convener and orchestrator while the Afghan parties occupy central stage, the United States will have more latitude to pursue its distinct national interests, largely behind the scenes.

To consolidate its interests through a peace accord, the United States must acknowledge that its interests may diverge in significant ways from its two nominal allies in the region, the Karzai government and the Pakistani government. Both of these actors may block a peace negotiation or subvert its implementation if they believe doing so is in their interest. The United States must be prepared to use the leverage and persuasion at its disposal if either does things that threaten American objectives. This leverage could include withholding aid, arms, and intelligence and engaging in unilateral military actions, if they are deemed necessary.

The American objective should be a stable and peaceful Afghanistan that neither hosts nor collaborates with international terrorists. Only to the extent that other issues impinge on this objective should American negotiators be drawn into a discussion of Afghanistan's social or constitutional issues. That qualification is significant, however, because constitutional issues will certainly affect Afghanistan's stability, as may social provisions if they are likely to antagonize influential elements of the population. In the end, however, Afghanistan's form of government and codes of behavior are preeminently of interest to the Afghans. Americans should have some confidence that a reasonably representative Afghan government delegation will not stray far from the desires of its population, the overwhelming majority of whom are strongly opposed to a return of an Islamic emirate and desirous of retaining the many gains they have made since 2001.

Iraq is an inexact parallel to the situation in Afghanistan, but several components of any peaceful solution in the latter are likely to be similar to those employed in the former. First, the United States will have to tolerate—indeed, seek to broker—the inclusion of former insurgents in an enlarged coalition government. Second, the United States will have to promise to "go home," withdrawing its remaining combat forces on a fixed, mutually agreed schedule (and subject to credible and verifiable measures showing that Afghanistan has not once again become a terrorist sanctuary). Third, Washington will need to remain heavily engaged in the implementation of whatever accord is reached.

We thus recommend that the United States seek the appointment of a UN-endorsed facilitator to promote agreement among all the necessary parties to an Afghan peace process regarding a venue, participation, and the agenda for talks. We believe that Germany (perhaps Bonn) might be a good locale for such talks, as might a site in Turkey. Alternatively, if the Taliban objects to a NATO locale, Doha and Geneva are neutral sites where the parties could conveniently converge. We recommend that only the Afghan parties take formal part in the core negotiations over their country's future but that all of the major external stakeholders, including India, Iran, Pakistan, Russia, and the United States, should conduct parallel, less formal discussions with a view to exercising convergent influence on the Afghan parties.

This monograph has illustrated the extreme complexity of any Afghan peace process. We believe, nevertheless, that a negotiated settlement is both feasible and desirable. However, success will require sustained and focused attention, from the American President on down. It will also require the whole-of-government approach that has become the hallmark of successful counterinsurgency. For the past several years, diplomacy and development have supported military operations in the effort to stabilize Afghanistan. This relationship will need to shift as a peace process gains momentum, with military operations increasingly supporting diplomacy by providing the leverage needed to bring adversaries to the table, the incentives needed to secure meaningful concessions, and the pacific gestures needed to reward constructive behavior.

References

Ahmad, Ishtiaq, "The U.S. Af-Pak Strategy: Challenges and Opportunities for Pakistan," *Asian Affairs: An American Review*, Vol. 37, 2010.

The Century Foundation—*See* The Century Foundation International Task Force on Afghanistan in Its Regional and Multilateral Dimensions.

The Century Foundation International Task Force on Afghanistan in Its Regional and Multilateral Dimensions, *Afghanistan, Negotiating Peace*, Washington, D.C., 2011.

Giustozzi, Antonio, *Empires of Mud: Wars and Warlords in Afghanistan*, New York: C. Hurst & Co. Ltd, 2009.

————, *Negotiating with the Taliban: Issues and Prospects*, Washington, D.C.: The Century Foundation, 2010.

iPOLL Databank, The Roper Center for Public Opinion Research, University of Connecticut, undated.

Järvenpää, Minna, "A Political Settlement in Afghanistan: Preparing for the Long Game, Not the End-Game," in Wolfgang Danspeckgruber, ed., *Working Toward Peace and Prosperity in Afghanistan*, Boulder, Colo.: Lynne Rienner Press, July 2010.

————, *Making Peace in Afghanistan: The Missing Political Strategy*, Washington, D.C.: United States Institute of Peace, Special Report No. 267, 2011.

Langer, Gary, "Afghanistan Poll: Where Things Stand 2010," ABCNews.com, November 30, 2010. As of July 10, 2011:
http://abcnews.go.com/Politics/Afghanistan/afghanistan-poll-things-stand-2010/story?id=12277743

Miller, Paul, "Finish the Job: How the War Can Still Be Won," *Foreign Affairs*, January/February 2011, pp. 56–57.

North Atlantic Treaty Organization, "Afghan National Security Forces (ANSF)," media backgrounder, March 2001.

Rubin, Alissa, "Afghan and Pakistani Leaders Meet in Peace Bid," *New York Times*, April 17, 2011, p. 8.

Ruttig, Thomas, *The Battle for Afghanistan: Negotiations with the Taliban*, Washington, D.C.: New America Foundation, May 23, 2011.

Semple, Michael, *Reconciliation in Afghanistan*, Washington, D.C.: United States Institute of Peace, 2009.

Shane, Scott, "Pakistan's Push on Afghan Peace Leaves U.S. Wary," *New York Times*, June 28, 2010.

Trenin, Dmitri, and Alexey Malashenko, *Afghanistan: A View from Moscow*, Washington, D.C.: Carnegie Endowment, 2010.

United Nations Assistance Mission in Afghanistan and Afghanistan Independent Human Rights Commission, *Afghanistan Annual Report 2010: Protection of Civilians in Armed Conflict*, Kabul, March 2011.

"Up to 35,000 Insurgents Active in Afghanistan: Official," *Peoples Daily Online*, February 9, 2011.

Waldman, Matt, *Dangerous Liaisons with the Afghan Taliban: The Feasibility and Risks of Negotiations*, Washington, D.C.: United States Institute of Peace, Special Report No. 256, 2010.

West, Bing, *The Wrong War: Grit, Strategy, and the Way Out of Afghanistan*, New York: Random House, 2011.

The White House, Office of the Press Secretary, "Remarks by President Obama at G-20 Press Conference in Toronto, Canada," June 27, 2010.